W9-ACD-724

A HOME ELSEWHERE

Based on The W. E. B. Du Bois Lectures

A HOME ELSEWHERE

READING AFRICAN AMERICAN CLASSICS IN THE AGE OF OBAMA

Robert B. Stepto

HARVARD UNIVERSITY PRESS

CAMBRIDGE, MASSACHUSETTS

LONDON, ENGLAND

2010

Library of Congress Cataloging-in-Publication Data
Stepto, Robert B.
A home elsewhere : reading African American classics in the age of Obama /
Robert B. Stepto.
(Based on the W. E. B. Du Bois lectures)
p. cm.
Includes bibliographical references and index.
ISBN 978-0-674-05096-9 (alk. paper)
1. American literature—African American authors—History and
criticism.   2. American literature—19th century—History and criticism.
3. American literature—20th century—History and criticism.   4. African
Americans—Intellectual life.   5. Identity (Psychology) in literature.
6. African Americans in literature.   I. Title.
PS153.N5S75 2010
810.9'896073—dc22
2010003532

for Gabriel, for Rafael

CONTENTS

Part One
The W. E. B. Du Bois Lectures

Part Two

A HOME ELSEWHERE

Part One

A Home Elsewhere:
Reading African American Classics
In the Age of Obama

INTRODUCTION

My topic in these lectures is "Reading the Classics (the African American Classics) in the Age of Obama." The idea for this came to me early in the fall of 2008 while I was writing the introduction for the new (2009) John Harvard Library edition of Frederick Douglass's 1845 *Narrative*. This was during the last weeks of the 2008 presidential campaign, and I couldn't help thinking about Douglass's *Narrative* and Obama's *Dreams from My Father* (1995) being first books, books that were black male bildungsromans, books that were unto themselves part of each man's effort to create a self and an identity. Other people were making their own connections. One colleague (my wife) talked about teaching *The Souls of Black Folk* during the run-up to the election and about how she and the students were mightily aware of how the discussion was being affected by the campaign. Articles started to appear that made connections as well, including, for example, David Samuels's piece on *Dreams from My Father* and Ralph Ellison's *Invisible Man* (*New Republic*, October 22, 2008). That reminded me of Leroi Jones's remarks in *The System of Dante's Hell* about black people being at once unseen yet constantly observed. Obama was in the mix of that, too. So I knew in broad terms that there was a project to pursue that involved being attentive to how we read African American literature at the present moment, knowing, and actually being stunned by the fact, that an African American *writer* is our president.

In all three talks I address Obama's *Dreams from My Father*, and in the second lecture I devote almost half my time to discussing scenes in that narrative. The first lecture, "Frederick Douglass, Barack Obama, and the Search for Patrimony," is an opportunity for me to discuss Douglass's work *My Bondage and My Freedom* (1855), the second and most personal of his autobiographies. In that lecture, I'm very interested in Douglass's discovery of a black father in Uncle Lawson, a man he meets and prays with in Baltimore. When Douglass tells us that he became determined to flee slavery once Uncle Lawson's dreams of freedom revisited him, he is indeed describing dreams from his father.

The second lecture, "W. E. B. Du Bois, Barack Obama, and the Search for Race," studies the schoolhouse episodes in *The Souls of Black Folk* (1903) and *Dreams from My Father*, which are early moments in the lives of both writers when they were schooled in race and taught that they were of a race. The lecture also examines schoolhouse episodes in James Weldon Johnson's *Autobiography of an Ex–Colored Man* (1911) and Zora Neale Hurston's *Their Eyes Were Watching God* (1937), novels that are, of course, African American classics as well. Throughout the discussion, I'm interested in how children negotiate their first moments of racial identity in school settings, and in the roles that adults do, and do not, play when children face their first racial crises.

The third lecture, "Toni Morrison, Barack Obama, and Difference," is my occasion to discuss Morrison's third novel, *Song of Solomon* (1977), which Mr. Obama listed as one of the books "most significant to him" in his correspondence with *Newsweek*'s Jon Meacham (Jon Meacham, "How to Read Like a President," *New York Times Book Review*, November 2, 2008). In Morrison's novel, Milkman Dead discovers that the song he keeps hearing—sometimes sung by children in their ring games—about Solomon flying home is actually a folk legend about his great-grandfather, Solomon, flying home to Africa. Not exactly in the song, however, is the fact that a wife and children were abandoned and left behind. The novel, in its array of characters, presents an array of family survivor stories. My discussion focuses (in its second half) on what several characters acquire, or think they need to acquire, in order to live with the pain of abandonment. Though it is not precisely a subject of my Morrison discussion, please assume that I couldn't write the piece without thinking to myself, as you perhaps are thinking: Barack Obama knows something about fathers flying off to Africa, and knows something about the temptation to create mythic stories about that fact in order to live with it.

Throughout the lectures, I return to several subjects: how protagonists raise themselves, often without one or both parents; how black boys invent black manhood, often with no examples or models before them; how protagonists seek and find a home elsewhere; and how protagonists create personalities that can deal with the pain of abandonment. These are age-old themes in African American literature that have a special poignancy and importance at the moment because our new, young, African American president has lived through these situations and circumstances and has written about them, notably in *Dreams from My Father.* Obama's narrative is a marvel in many ways; these include the ways it refreshes our readings and recollections of the whole of African American literature.

An earlier version of the second Du Bois lecture was offered as the 2009 Abernethy Lecture at Middlebury College. I thank my hosts at Harvard and at Middlebury for their support and many courtesies.

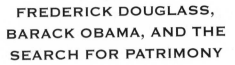

1

FREDERICK DOUGLASS, BARACK OBAMA, AND THE SEARCH FOR PATRIMONY

I looked for *home* elsewhere

—Frederick Douglass,
My Bondage and My Freedom (1855)

In one of the "Origins" chapters in *Dreams from My Father,* Barack Obama writes about the miseries of being a fifteen-year-old whose adolescent anxieties are compounded by issues of identity and race. In describing what he calls his "fitful interior struggle," he writes, "I was trying to raise myself to be a black man in America, and beyond the given of my appearance, no one around me seemed to know exactly what that meant."[1] Adolescence is often remembered as a time of being alone in the world; Obama's personal expression of that sentiment is striking because it so clearly alludes to the absence of his black father and to the irrelevance, given the issues at hand, of his white mother and grandparents. Gender is obviously part of the dilemma—he states specifically that he is trying to raise himself to be a black man—and so it is not surprising that he latches on to two engrossing pursuits: basketball, which is physical, communal, and arguably fraternal, and the reading of classics of African American literature by male authors, which may or may not be a fraternal activity, but most certainly is for the young Obama a private, mental activity best pursued alone in one's bedroom.

Regarding the basketball obsession, the adult Obama is quick to admit that it was a bit of a pose: "I was living out a caricature of black male adolescence, itself a caricature of swaggering American manhood" (D 79), observing that he and most of the "man-boys" around him were choosing "a costume, armor against uncertainty" (79–80). But perhaps there is something deeply personal involved as well: his basketball was a Christmas gift from his father, his missing black father. It is what he has from the last time (which was, in ways, the first time) he saw him.

Obama's reading is a closed-door, surreptitious pursuit, no doubt because he's anxious about what his grandparents might think of what he is reading. He writes, "I gathered up books from the library—Baldwin, Ellison, Hughes, Wright, Du Bois. At night I would close the door to my room, telling my grandparents I had homework to do, and there I would sit and wrestle with words, locked in suddenly desperate argument, trying to reconcile the world as I'd found it with the terms of my birth" (D 85). At fifteen, Obama found these writers unhelpful: "In every page in every book, in Bigger Thomas and invisible men [note Obama's plural], I kept finding the same anguish, the same doubt; a self-contempt that neither irony nor intellect seemed able to deflect" (85–86). The only book that "seemed to offer something different" was *The Autobiography of Malcolm X*. Obama recalls admiring the "blunt poetry" of Malcolm's prose and "his unadorned insistence on respect." And he adds this praise: "His [Malcolm's] repeated acts of self-creation spoke to me" (86). Malcolm did indeed invent himself as a black man more than once; there is much to learn in that, including the fact that self-creation may need to be repeated.

Obama's desire for "repeated acts of self-creation," including writerly acts of self-creation, must be understood in terms of how the created self attaches to community, and is in a real sense fully created through that attachment. This is why he would be attracted to Malcolm's narrative and disappointed by, say, Ellison's *Invisible Man*. For example, I can imagine Obama being fascinated by the Vet's advice to Invisible Man, "Be your own father," but appalled by the thought that what that leads to is, perchance, a semisane existence in an urban basement "shut off and forgotten in the nineteenth century."[2]

As I muse on who, in addition to Malcolm, might have riveted Obama, I'm drawn to considering that he might have found much to ponder in the autobiographical writings of Frederick Douglass, particularly *My Bondage and My Freedom* (1855). At fifteen, young Obama might well have scoffed at the idea of reading Douglass; he might have argued to himself that he needed to be reading today's writers, writers addressing the here and now of what he, Obama, was living. But Douglass's writings of 150 years ago have much to offer, especially to someone with the issues Obama has wrestled with. Douglass's autobiography is preeminently about raising himself and becoming a black man in America, most certainly while living with no one who "seemed to know exactly what that meant." Douglass has his own particular concerns not just with claiming his masculinity but also with seeking out a plausible and liveable biracial masculinity. Moreover, after being completely orphaned at an early age, Douglass's raising of himself is a tale of finding a "home elsewhere," of forming communities of friends and lingering in those moments when a man or woman offers something approaching paternal or maternal succor. In *My Bondage and My Freedom,* Douglass presents what David Samuels describes (in writing about Obama alone) as "the personality created to deal with the pain of abandonment."[3] It is with these thoughts especially in view that I would like to offer an "age-of-Obama assessment" of Douglass's most personal autobiography.

A striking feature of Douglass's opening chapters in *My Bondage and My Freedom* is that slavery is first vilified for its corrosions of the slave family. We meet Betsey and Isaac Baily, the grandparents with whom the young boy Douglass lives, who have a cabin of their own apart from the other slave cabins and who maintain an admired domestic order and industry. This may suggest a modicum of independence from the slave system, but in fact the Baily household is indispensable to the system since, Grandmother Betsey's real task is to take in and take care of the children of her five daughters, one of whom, Harriet, is Douglass's mother. This obviously assists the slaveholders in their schemes of hiring out the daughters for labor on distant farms while providing a nursery, which is in truth an orphanage, for the new "crop" of slave children. In short, the grandmother's role is to be complicit in "obliterating . . . all just ideas of the sacredness of the family"[4] while caretaking a semblance of the family.

Grandfather Isaac is not mentioned or named in Douglass's 1845 *Narrative,* so he is a new character to readers only familiar with that earlier version of Douglass's story. Perhaps he doesn't appear in the 1845 *Narrative* because he was such a "present absence" in Douglass's young life. The skills at fishing and assembling fishing nets and at growing vegetables are Grandmother Betsey's, not his. And the five daughters who have borne all those children are consistently referred to as grandmother's daughters. So what do we know about Isaac? We know that he is free, and we sense that he might be the only free black man in young Douglass's immediate world. Douglass himself must have wondered, as we do, how Grandfather Isaac could be free and such a nonentity. Perhaps he grew into an understanding of how slavery might successfully render a free black man (and father) nonexistent. I would like to think that Isaac became for Douglass what Richard Wright termed "a warning not an example." Which is to say, that when Douglass self-created himself as a free black man, he would do everything he could to be free but not on the terms imposed on Grandfather Isaac.

As Douglass grows older, he slowly learns that the dear old cabin is not owned by his grandparents but by a distant, mysterious figure known as "Old Master." Moreover, he learns that "Old Master" owns Grandmother Betsey, and all the children in her care, including, of course, Douglass himself. Most sobering is the piece of news that once a child is "big enough," he or she must leave "Grand-mammy" to go to live at "Old Master's." In this manner, Douglass poignantly informs us that the greatest horror slavery presented to him as a young child was the "liability," as he calls it, but in truth the inevitability, of being separated from his grandmother, "seldom or never to see her again" (MB 39).

As likely as the separation is, we are nonetheless stunned when the event occurs, principally because of the grandmother's role in delivering Douglass to what he calls the "realities of slavery." The whole of chapter 2 of *My Bondage,* significantly entitled "The Author Removed from His Home," is devoted to the long, twelve-mile walk he makes with his grandmother, through "somber woods" in which logs and stumps impose and at times appear to be wild beasts, to arrive at "old master's" plantation. This, too, is the Grandmother's duty to perform in the slave system, and the only maternal gesture she can manage in this work is to kindly not tell young Douglass where they are headed.

What she does tell him, once they arrive at "Old Master's," is that all the children running about—"black, brown, copper colored and nearly white," as Douglass observes—are kin to him. Some are cousins, and three of them, Perry, Sarah, and Eliza, are his siblings. But all are strangers, children Douglass has vaguely heard of but never seen before, and he rightly fears that playing with them, which his Grandmother is urging, will produce the very moment in which she vanishes from his life. What the scene presents so clearly is the drama in which the slave family enacts its scripted destruction. Words like "home" and "brother" and "sister" are known but stripped of meaning and, worse, become words to distrust. Late in the afternoon, a child (could it be a brother? a sister?) rushes up to Douglass and, with "a sort of roguish glee," exclaims, " 'Fed, Fed! grand-mammy gone! Grand-mammy gone!' " (MB 49). He is, of course, devastated. When he later observes that he had never been deceived before, we sense that he speaks not just of his Grandmother but of the whole grand deception that all his kin have had a role in, and into which they as slaves were born.

Later in *My Bondage,* Douglass provides the almost requisite scenes of savage beatings and the like (including the legendary whipping of his Aunt Hester by her master, Capt. Anthony), but he begins his story with this particular "scene of subjection,"[5] his arrival at "Old Master's" place. Surely one reason he does so is so that he might clarify how the quest for a home elsewhere was instigated for him by abandonment and by a growing awareness that he would have to invent that home, as well as the family that composed home. Freedom would include the task of becoming a kinsman and a black man the likes of whom Douglass had not seen or lived with.

In *Dreams from My Father,* Obama writes at one point about packing attributes into his father's image. In *My Bondage,* Douglass pursues a similar activity in portraying his mother, and for the same reason: inventing or imaging a missing parent is a needful component of self-creation. And we note in each case that it is the black parent whom the biracial child is assembling. Obama doesn't bother much with assembling his white parent, his mother, precisely because she was, as he puts it, the "single constant" in his life. For Douglass, his white father was the absolute opposite of a "constant" in his life: he was a mystery, never to be seen or named, for indeed, "Slavery does away with fathers, as it does away with families" (MB 51). The one attribute, other than race, that Douglass lends to his father is the suggestion that he was at least good enough not to sell his son far away.

In Douglass's own words, whereas his father was a "mystery," his mother became a "myth." Orphaned in that manner, Douglass had no "intelligible beginning in the world" (MB 60). With utter candor, he tells us that in order to have a mother to remember he had to create her: "I had to learn the value of my mother long after her death, and by witnessing the devotion of other mothers to their children" (60). The crowning event in his myth of his mother is her visit to "Old Master's" place on one of days when the oppressive Aunt Katy (clearly the evil stepmother in this tale) is punishing young Douglass by not feeding him. Outraged, his mother reads "aunt Katy a lecture which she never forgot" (56) and gives her boy not the hoped-for slice of cornbread but a ginger cake, in the shape of a heart. Douglass remembers her as being, then, a mother who was "more than a match for all his enemies" (56). He concludes, "That night I learned the fact, that I was not only a child, but *somebody's* child" (56).

If the crowning event is the "blessing out" of Aunt Katy, the crowning attribute is the mother's ability to read, which Douglass learns of only after her death. Apparently, "she was the *only* one of all the slaves and colored people in Tuckahoe who enjoyed that advantage" (MB 58). This information nicely enhances the "myth" of the mother while building Douglass's own self-creation story as well: in creating himself as a literate black man he can point to a genealogy, if you will, of black literacy. Douglass enthuses about this in just this way:

> That a "field hand" should learn to read, in any slave state, is remarkable; but the achievement of my mother, considering the place, was extraordinary; and, in view of that fact, I am quite

willing, even happy, to attribute any love of letters I possess, and for which I have got—despite of prejudices—only too much credit, *not* to my admitted Anglo-Saxon paternity, but to the native genius of my sable, unprotected, and uncultivated *mother*—a woman who belonged to a race whose mental endowments it is, at present, fashionable to hold in disparagement and contempt. (58)

Douglass and his mother, Harriet, were apart during her last long illness as well as during her last few hours of life. There was no opportunity or effort made for a slave boy to see his dying mother. When word came of her death, Douglass tells us that he received the tidings with "no strong emotions of sorrow for her, and with very little regret for myself on account of her loss" (60). The simple fact of the matter was that he didn't know her: during the years he lived with his Grandmother he never once saw his mother; during his time at "Old Master's," his visits with her were so few and so spare that he did not even know that she could read. He would only get to know her when he created her, and when he assigned to his memory of her an image he found, in a book.

While it is not often put this way, the rest of Douglass's childhood is a story of occasional maternal gestures from white women and, once in Baltimore, a biracial boy's longing for a black father. The first of the white women is Miss Lucretia Auld, for whom young Douglass runs occasional errands. While he goes out of his way to say that she was not especially attentive to him, he stresses that, in the context of slavery, her human kindness was a rare boon, and one that she extended to him alone among the slave children. As he puts it, Miss Lucretia "bestowed upon me such words and looks as taught me that she pitied me, if she did not love me. In addition to words and looks, she sometimes gave me a piece of bread and butter" (MB 130). In due time, young Douglass discovers that if he stops and sings a tune beneath Miss Lucretia's window, more bread and butter will be his reward. Like his mother, Miss Lucretia, in great contrast to the evil Aunt Katy, is the woman who feeds him, and in that way variously nourishes him. She is also the kind soul who attends to young Douglass's wounds after he's been in a nasty fight with a boy named Ike. Aunt Katy, we are told, "paid no attention either to my wound or to my roaring, except to tell me that it served me right" (130). Miss Lucretia, however, called him into the parlor (a visit Douglass describes as "an extra privilege unto itself") and "quietly acted the good Samaritan" (130). Starved for kindness and a mother's touch, Douglass recalls Miss Lucretia's attentions in minute detail:

> With her own soft hand she washed the blood from my head and face, Fetched her own balsam bottle, and with the balsam wetted a nice piece of white linen, and bound up my head. The balsam was not more healing to the wound in my head, than her kindness was healing to the wounds in my spirit, made by the unfeeling words of Aunt Katy. After this, Miss Lucretia was my friend. I felt her to be such; and I have no doubt that the simple act of binding up my head, did much to awaken in her mind an interest in my welfare. (130–131)

This suggests that Miss Lucretia may have had a role in young Douglass, of all the slave children, being selected to go to Baltimore in the privileged position of companion to the son of Hugh and Sophia Auld, Miss Lucretia's in-laws.

While Douglass never determines to what extent Miss Lucretia might have instigated his assignment to Baltimore, which is the most significant thing that happens to him as a boy, he does know that she is the kind one among the "harsh, cold and indifferent" slaveholders, and that she is the one who prepares him, as a mother would, for his new life in the city. It is she who, for example, urges Douglass to wash himself thoroughly, to scrub away the dead skin and mange of slavery, and it is she who promises the freshly groomed boy his first pair of trousers. One could say that Miss Lucretia simply doesn't want to send to her Baltimore in-laws a slave boy who is dirty and ragged, but Douglass recalls the matter as a kindness to him. Indeed, for Douglass, Miss Lucretia is forever to be associated with the opportunity to go to Baltimore, especially after he becomes her property at age eleven and is sent back to the city again, presumably by her.

Douglass's other "white mother" is Sophia Auld, his Baltimore mistress. She enters the story right after Douglass surveys the wreckage of his family in Tuckahoe and utters so poignantly, "I looked for home elsewhere" (MB 135). Eventually, Sophia Auld becomes Exhibit A for how slavery victimizes the slaveholder and slave alike, but in the beginning she is a good woman whom Douglass cannot help but describe in tender, maternal terms. Quite significantly, he tells us that in Miss Sophia's household he is suddenly a person: "I had been treated as a *pig* on the plantation; I was treated as a *child* now" (142). He adds, "I therefore soon learned to regard her as something more akin to a mother, than a slaveholding mistress" (142). And he portrays this special scene:

> If little Thomas was her son, and her most dearly beloved child, she, for a time, at least, made me something like his half-brother in her affections. If dear Tommy was exalted to a place on his mother's knee, "Feddy" was honored by a place at his mother's side. Nor did he lack the caressing strokes of her gentle hand, to convince him that, though *motherless,* he was not *friendless.* (143)

It is in the midst of such affection that young Douglass asks Miss Sophia to teach him to read, and she "without hesitation" begins the lessons.

What soon transpires is one of the most well-known of Douglass's childhood stories: Mr. Hugh Auld, Sophia's husband, learns of the lessons and abruptly ends them, saying famously, among other things, "If you give a nigger an inch, he will take an ell"; "he should know nothing but the will of his master, and learn to obey it." "Learning will spoil the best nigger in the world"; "if you teach that nigger—speaking of myself—how to read the bible, there will be no keeping him" (MB 146). Douglass hears these remarks and declares them "the first decidedly anti-slavery lecture to which it had been my lot to listen" (146). Later, he proclaims that with this new knowledge of "the white man's power to perpetuate the enslavement of the black man" he now "understood the direct pathway from slavery to freedom" (146–147).

This is a familiar passage with most of its language taken verbatim from Douglass's rendering of the event in the 1845 *Narrative*. Yet it reads in a fresh way in *My Bondage* precisely because this is the autobiography in which Douglass has already told us that his mother could read, and so we cannot help but wonder what may be pursued or enacted in the reading lessons with Miss Sophia. One thing is sure: Miss Sophia is the mother who reads who teaches him how to read. In this regard, the intimacy of lessons, however short-lived, is a repair of abandonment. We know that reading will be Douglass's bond with his mother. It should also be seen as the means by which he will avoid for himself the lot that befell his mother.

Douglass finds his black father figure in Baltimore in Uncle Lawson, a devout, prayerful man whose "words, (when he spoke to his friends,) were about a better world" (MB 167). What Uncle Lawson offers is the friendship of an older man and a fellowship in Christ: Douglass revels in how they are a great help to each other, with him helping Uncle Lawson with his reading, and Uncle Lawson teaching him the spirit. What that spirit entails is just enough of what today would be called liberationist theology for Douglass to become commited to raising himself to be a useful man with great work to do in *this* world. Douglass and Lawson enjoy their singing, prayers, and lessons in Lawson's home, which is near the Auld residence. They thus created for themselves the beginnings of what a certain Chicago preacher told Mr. Obama he needed: a "church home." Douglass goes to Uncle Lawson's home every chance he gets; especially after Miss Sophia's reading lessons end, it seems to be a "home elsewhere." Not surprisingly, Mr. Auld, who forbade the reading lessons, soon forbids the visits to Uncle Lawson. Apparently, home, or a home in faith, will also "spoil the best nigger in the world." Auld's threats strengthen Douglass's faith and determination, including his faith in Uncle Lawson's certainty that "the Lord can make you free."

Over the course of his recollections of Uncle Lawson, Douglass subtly shifts from calling him "Uncle" to referring to him as "father." At one point, Lawson is Douglass's "spiritual father" whom he loves intensely (MB 168); at another point, he is his "dear old father." Late in *My Bondage,* Douglass contends that the dreams of freedom that lead him to bond with black brethren and to plot an escape from slavery are from "Father Lawson":

> You may hurl a man so low, beneath the level of his kind, that he loses all just ideas of his natural position; but elevate him a little, and the clear conception of rights rises to life and power, and leads him onward. Thus elevated, a little, at Freeland's, the dreams called into being by that great good man, Father Lawson, when in Baltimore, began to visit me; and the shoots from the tree of liberty began to put forth tender buds, and dim hopes of the future began to dawn. (263–264)

These dreams are, for Douglass, "dreams from my father." Uncle Lawson is not just the father Douglass finds but the father he needs. He is another marker of possibility and hope that a young slave can find in the city, as opposed to the plantation. This is abundantly clear if one compares Uncle Lawson to his plantation counterpart on "Old Master's" place. In the city, you find pious Lawson, and you can "refresh" yourself with him in shared song and prayer; on the plantation, you discover Uncle Isaac Copper, the slave who whips the slave children as they learn the Lord's Prayer, thus proving, in Douglass's words, that "Everybody, in the South, wants the privilege of whipping somebody else" (70).

In *Dreams from My Father*, Obama describes his earliest attraction to playing basketball in this way: "At least on the basketball court I could find a community of sorts, with an inner life all its own. It was there that I would make my closest white friends. . . . And it was there that I would meet Ray and the other blacks close to my age who had begun to trickle into the islands" (D 80). In *My Bondage*, young Douglass reaches an age where he gives up completely on finding succor in the Auld household and seeks out Uncle Lawson as well as a community of boys: "My attachments were now outside of our family. They were felt to those [young colored men] to whom I *imparted* instruction, and to those little white boys from whom I *received* instruction" (MB 183). In each instance, we see our authors discovering at a young age that finding community is a stay against the confusions and hurts of fractured family life. The communities found seem to provide respite from the confusions of race as well. Obama suggests that on the courts boys of different races could, at times, simply be boys. Douglass's embrace of white boys among his "attachments" reminds us of his first description of the boys who taught him, which includes this remark: "I do not remember ever to have met with a boy, while I was in slavery, who defended the slave system; but I have often had boys to console me, with the hope that something yet would occur, by which I might be made free" (156). In these communities, which are in truth fraternities, a kind of biracial selfhood is possible, when that is desirable.

For Douglass, forging fraternity soon is of a piece with raising himself to be a man of God, and this leads to his years of attending, and eventually leading, Sabbath schools. The first school he leads, or helps lead, is back at St. Michael's, on the Eastern Shore, where he has been returned after the death of Miss Lucretia. It forms when a Mr. Wilson, the one white man in the district not against imparting lessons to slaves, invites Douglass to assist him in teaching a Sabbath school at the house of James Mitchell, a free colored man. Douglass is ecstatic: "Here, thought, I, is something worth living for; here is an excellent chance for usefulness; and I shall soon have a company of young friends, lovers of knowledge, like some of my Baltimore friends, from whom I now felt parted forever" (MB 200). The school lasts exactly one Sunday; at the second meeting, a white mob, led by at least two Methodist "class-leaders," violently breaks up the lessons. We don't learn what happened to Mr. Wilson or James Mitchell. For his part, Douglass is accused of wanting to be another Nat Turner, and is warned that if he keeps it up, he will be shot as many times as Turner.

Douglass's next opportunity to start a Sabbath school comes during his time on Mr. Freeland's plantation. These are the months of planning the escape attempt involving a small band of black brethren, for each of whom Douglass is to write a protection, and the Sabbath school plays no small role in creating this fellowship for freedom. When the school commences, the lessons are held outdoors, in a manner mindful of what is described in Paul Laurence Dunbar's poem "Ante-Bellum Sermon." Two of the first scholars are Henry and John Harris, brothers who are best friends of Douglass and will be in that number of dedicated souls planning to escape at Eastertide.

Soon, Douglass has a brotherhood, "twenty or thirty young men, who enrolled themselves, gladly, in my Sabbath school, and were willing to meet with me regularly, under the trees or elsewhere, for the purpose of learning to read" (MB 265). They read, they speak openly among themselves about freedom, and they bond, as Douglass reports:

> For much of the happiness—or absence of misery—with which I passed this year with Mr. Freeland, I am indebted to the genial temper and ardent friendship of my brother slaves. They were, every one of them, manly, generous and brave, yes; I say they were brave, and I will add, fine looking. It is seldom the lot of mortals to have truer and better friends than were the slaves on this farm. It is not uncommon to charge slaves with great treachery toward each other, and to believe them incapable of confiding in each other; but I must say, that I never loved, esteemed, or confided in men, more than I did in these. They were as true as steel, and no band of brothers could have been more loving. (268–269)

In this and similar passages, Douglass is clear about how difficult and painful it is to entertain the thought that he and his small band were betrayed by a slave on Freeland's farm. Even when several factors point to Sandy Jenkins (the slave who dropped out of the plan at the last moment) as the betrayer, Douglass tells us, "We all loved him too well to think it *possible* that he could have betrayed us" (MB 297).

The outcome of the betrayal is that Douglass not only loses a chance for freedom but also loses his fraternity of friends. At first, Douglass and the Harris brothers and the rest of the band (slaves named Charles Roberts and Henry Baily) are one in their solidarity and denials of intent. They are also one when they are dragged fifteen miles and summarily thrown in jail. Then, separation arrives by degree: they are divided and incarcerated in two different cells, and then, after the Easter holidays, Messrs. Freeland and Hamilton arrive to take away all of the accused except Douglass. Of this, Douglass writes, "I was now left entirely alone in prison. The innocent had been taken, and the guilty left. My friends were separated from me, and apparently forever" (MB 300). Douglass was left in jail alone another week, tormented by thoughts of the "living death" awaiting him, away from his friends, "beset with the innumerable horrors of the cotton field, and the sugar plantation," that seemed his likely doom (302). He was no doubt tormented as well by the question of whether, if released, he could ever create himself again.

After the week, Thomas Auld shows up to release Douglass, claiming that his plan is to send Douglass to Alabama with a friend of his, who will emancipate him at the end of eight years. Being sent to Alabama is the only part of this tale Douglass half-believes. When the Alabama friend never appears, events take a near-miraculous turn, and Douglass is sent back to Baltimore to the Hugh Auld household. Nearly three years later, it will be from Baltimore that Douglass will successfully escape to freedom on a date he can name, read, and write: September 3, 1838.

Douglass's escape north by train, under the assumed identity of a sailor whose papers he possesses, gets him to New York. While pretending to be a sailor with a paper protection can be seen as a vestige of the original plot to escape by sea, gone is the determination to escape within a community of stalwart friends. He has created the self who can do this alone. Of his first days in New York, with nowhere to go, nowhere to sleep safely, and no one to turn to until he meets up by chance with another fugitive from Baltimore named Jake, Douglass writes, unforgettably: "I was not only free from slavery, but I was free from home as well" (MB 340). Now that he was "elsewhere," he needed to form a self and "home elsewhere."

A feature of this activity is the quick succession of names Douglass assumes over the course of traveling from Baltimore to New York, and eventually on to New Bedford. Upon leaving Baltimore, he is no longer "Frederick Bailey" but "Stanley," which is likely the name of the sailor he is impersonating. Once in New York, and indisputably a *fugitive* slave, he renames himself "Frederick Johnson," no doubt to throw slave-catchers off the track of "Bailey" or "Stanley." And then in New Bedford, at the suggestion of Nathan Johnson, a free colored man, who has been reading Walter Scott's *Lady of the Lake,* Douglass becomes, on his first morning in New England, "Frederick Douglass." These name changes were a key strategy in Douglass's successful escape plan, but they also put in plain view his initial efforts to invent the self he hoped to become. The change from "Frederick Johnson" to "Frederick Douglass" is especially revealing. As a "Johnson," Douglass disappeared for a time into the masses of colored men named "Johnson," free in a kind of anonymity or invisibility. As Douglass, he steps forth into a new name, for a new world; it is a name from literature, the name of a leader and a king; it is a name that can be, for Douglass, something other than a slave name. It can be a name to be handed down.

Names are handed down in families, and family has been as elusive as home in Douglass's life story. It is therefore quite revealing that within days of arriving to New York, he is joined there by Anna Murray, a free woman from Baltimore. They are married by Rev. James W. C. Pennington on September 15, just twelve days after Douglass has escaped slavery and the South. Clearly, this part of the plan for a new life was in place before many others: Douglass did not know, for example, that he was going to start a family in New Bedford, but he did know he was going to start it with Anna Murray, whom he had met at meetings of the East Baltimore Mental Improvement Society. The liberty Douglass hoped for included the liberty to be a husband

and father. Having a family was a way of saying that he was free of slavery even if he was not free.

I think that President Obama would agree that Douglass, in leading Sabbath schools in the South and in becoming an antislavery agent in the North, was something of a community organizer. Of course, the objectives were different: leading a Sabbath school was organizing for self-help, and agitating for abolition was organizing for a movement. But seen in personal terms, a common thread in this work for Douglass was finding community and fraternity as part of the process of creating one's self and one's manhood. This was somewhat easier to do in the context of the Sabbath school, despite the intrusions of slavery, because Douglass's position as a leader and brother was clear: he was the one who had been schooled in faith and freedom in Father Lawson's home; he was the one who could read and write. Finding community and self in the abolitionist community was harder at times because Douglass's position in the cause was often under review, and not always all that he hoped it would be. This was especially true in the early 1840s, when Douglass was an agent for the Garrisonian abolitionists who first embraced him and gave him a career. When Douglass arrived to the North, he knew something about the white boys of Baltimore who opposed slavery, but he had much to learn about the white men of Boston who called themselves abolitionists.

As we know from recent election history, people do try to impose their own scripts on black leaders, including scripts for how they might become the leaders they don't plan to be. Talking points are included along with advice about appearance, comportment, articulateness, and anger management for all. In the case of Douglass, after he had been speaking on the circuit for three months and was beginning to chafe at telling the same personal story again and again, the advice from the abolitionists was "Let us have the facts"; "Give us the facts, we will take care of the

philosophy"; "Tell your story"; "Better have a little of the plantation manner of speech than not; 'tis best that you not seem too
learned" (MB 361–362). There was no room in the script either
for Douglass's ideas or for his "moral indignation." There was no
room for him to grow, especially on his own terms.

African American physician James McCune Smith, in his introduction to the original 1855 edition of *My Bondage*, described the Garrisonian abolitionists in these pungent terms:
"these gentlemen, although proud of Frederick Douglass, failed
to fathom, and bring out to the light of day, the highest qualities of his mind; the force of their own education stood in their
own way: they did not delve into the mind of a colored man for
capacities which the pride of race led them to believe to be re-
stricted to their own Saxon blood" (xxii). On the matter of their
script for Douglass, Smith added: "Bitter and vindictive sarcasm,
irresistible mimicry, and a pathetic narrative of his own experiences of slavery, were the intellectual manifestations which they
encouraged him to exhibit on the platform or in the lecture
desk" (xxii). If Douglass did not perform this idea of Negro,
his abolitionist friends declared that he would be branded
"uppity."

What Douglass encountered was paternalism; a paternalism
imposed on him, and a paternalism that, to some degree, he
sought. On the one hand, the abolitionists wanted Douglass to
be forever the boy, their boy, whom they discovered at a Nan-
tucket meeting in 1841, and they were disappointed that he
grew and breached that role. On the other hand, Douglass
could not help seeking at first, in William Lloyd Garrison especially, another father figure like Father Lawson, who could fill a
void and guide him in the cause and righteousness of emancipa-
tion. As the abolitionists became disappointed in him, Douglass
in turn became disappointed in them. He sought a paternalism
that nurtured, not one that, increasingly, merely commanded.

I review this part of Douglass's story to portray these abolitionists not as bad men but as American men, and to show Douglass as an American man among them. Community is hard to find and hard to maintain. People trying to do good, even when trying to do so in the name of human brotherhood, nonetheless enact race rituals and racial behaviors that seem at times to be hardwired. And betrayals, large and small, appear in every quarter. Douglass was likely betrayed by abolitionists; he was certainly betrayed by whoever exposed the escape plans of 1836. Just as Douglass had to create a personality to deal with the pain of abandonment, he also had to create a self who could deal with the pain of betrayal. Dealing with either pain requires the same inner strength, for indeed, abandonment is betrayal, and betrayal is abandonment.

James McCune Smith argues that the secret of Douglass's power is that he is a "Representative American man—a type of his countryman" (MB xxv), and I concur with that conclusion. The heart of Smith's argument is that, to the fullest extent, "Frederick Douglass has passed through every gradation of rank comprised in our national make-up, and bears upon his person and upon his soul everything that is American" (xxv). To that I would add that Douglass is representative in confronting the challenges particular to the nation in creating a self, finding a family, and finding a home elsewhere. The fact that he wrote about these challenges, understanding that that, too, could be essential to creating the self, also renders him "a type of his countryman." It places Douglass in a tradition of American writing that is still valued and sustained by many fine writers today, including the forty-fourth president of the United States.

W. E. B. DU BOIS, BARACK OBAMA, AND THE SEARCH FOR RACE

School House Blues

> Everybody remembers the first time they were *taught* that part
> of the human race was Other. That's a trauma. It's as though I
> told you that your left hand is not part of your body.
>
> —Toni Morrison[1]

The schoolhouse episode is a staple event in African American narratives no doubt because it is remembered or imagined as a formative first scene of racial self-awareness.[1] It is not a moment when race is adopted—that may come later; it is instead a moment when race is imposed. The episode may involve a graduation exercise, with all the attendant questions regarding what, exactly, is commencing. Though set in a hotel ballroom, the battle royal in the first chapter of Ralph Ellison's *Invisible Man* is one such monumental episode. More likely, though, the episode is an earlier moment, perhaps the first day of school, in which the narrative's protagonist is "schooled" in being colored, sometimes made aware for the first time that he or she is colored. Obama's *Dreams from My Father* offers a schoolhouse episode that is singular in its complexity, partly because it is a series of evolving scenes and because the events are complicated by the presence of family members—Obama's white Kansan grandfather and black Kenyan father in particular—who hover and haunt and literally enter the schoolhouse during Obama's first weeks in an American classroom. (He had been in school in

Indonesia before.) These features of the episode, which takes up most of the narrative's chapter 3, render Obama's version of the schoolhouse story virtually unique. Even so, his story is of a piece with the stories that have come before: these are stories about the onslaught of insult and difference, about young people first becoming aware of how unaware they are of themselves in the world.

Before discussing the schoolhouse episode in *Dreams from My Father*, I would like to review certain features of the episodes famously offered by W. E. B. Du Bois, James Weldon Johnson, and Zora Neale Hurston. Each of these episodes occurs in the opening pages of a canonical African American text; each has features that direct us to assessing particular attributes of Obama's chapter. Let me begin with the visiting-card affair right at the beginning of Du Bois's *Souls of Black Folk* (1903).

Given the fact that Du Bois was writing during terrible times for the American Negro, a period historian Rayford Logan called "the nadir" of African American history,[2] it is striking that he begins *Souls* with an incident of insult, not atrocity, set among the green hills of New England's Berkshires, not the red clay of the South's Cotton Belt.

In his opening sentences, Du Bois presents a "wee wooden schoolhouse" and describes himself as "a little thing," clearly suggesting the young, naïve innocence of the self and circumstance to be sullied. What happened that fateful day, "when the shadow swept across me," was at first just an occasion of childish frivolity: "something put it into the boys' and girls' heads to buy gorgeous visiting-cards—ten cents a package—and exchange."[3] "The exchange was merry," Du Bois recalls, "till one girl, a tall newcomer, refused my card,—refused it peremptorily, with a glance" (S 38).

There is something to observe in almost every word offered

in this passage of remembrance. The "shadow" that sweeps across Du Bois prefigures his famous trope of the Veil, which is variously that which shuts him (and others) out of "their world," that which he himself can put in place in seeking a self-protective isolation, and that which he will triumphantly live above, in time. But first, it is a shadow, rendering him a shadow. One notes that the visiting-cards are "gorgeous" and that they were, for a boy whose only meager funds came from the occasional odd job, costly: "ten cents a package."

Anger is expressed in that detail: even as an adult, Du Bois is still seething about actually having paid good money for what happened to him. The girl is not named, perhaps because Du Bois wishes to expose the behavior of a whole class of people, not that of one individual alone. She is described as a "tall newcomer." It has been appropriately suggested that in this remark Du Bois is retaliating by "othering" the girl as one of the new immigrant girls.[4] "Tall" is an interesting detail as well, since we know that Du Bois was short. What rage (and contempt) is thus expressed in characterizing the girl as "new" and "tall," the point being that is it rage of this order that must be controlled and channeled into the special energy and dedication that brings the sunny days with "bluest" skies when "the strife [is] . . . fiercely sunny" (S 38).

"Refused" is twice written, lingered over, and then modified by "peremptorily," the very sort of two-dollar word Du Bois spelled correctly "when I could beat my mates at examination-time." The card is refused "with a glance," and that is a key to the scene. What happened to Du Bois that day was that he was initiated into double-consciousness, which is precisely the "peculiar sensation" of "looking at one's self through the eyes of others." And so Du Bois directs us to the tall girl's eyes and instructs us in the pain that even a glance can inflict. Even a merry moment in a New England schoolhouse can be what Saidiya Hartman has termed a "scene of subjection."

Du Bois revels in beating his fellow students in examinations and in footraces, adding that beating "their stringy heads" was pretty good, too. Yet he calls them his mates, which suggests that an allegiance exists along with the animosity. This expresses a two-ness that is mirrored in how Du Bois situates himself with other black youth, or, more precisely, other black boys. He refers to "us" and includes himself among the "sons of night," but he is the one who knows the light of the "bluest" days. He is determined not to be of that black number whose "youth shrunk into tasteless sycophancy, or into silent hatred of the pale world . . . or wasted itself in a bitter cry" (S 38). Life above the Veil is, in short, life above a lot of people of many circumstances, which suggests that seeking the true self-consciousness that lies beyond, or above, double-consciousness can be a self-isolating activity, or is necessarily self-isolating. Du Bois does indeed appear to be alone in his schoolhouse episode. There are no adults, not even a teacher; no students have names or otherwise materialize as individuals except the tall newcomer girl. "Other black boys" are cited in the episode's paragraph but not explicitly as fellow students, and no one black boy emerges as a friend or a relative with a name, or as a knowing compatriot who shares the strife. In short, Du Bois's "we" contains a lot of "me;" filling "we" with "me" is something that began that day in the "wee schoolhouse."

James Weldon Johnson's young colored male in *The Autobiography of an Ex-Colored Man* (1912) also attends public school in a New England schoolhouse. In this instance, the hero narrator lives and attends school in Connecticut, not Massachusetts, which puts him and his mother close enough to New York so that, on at least one occasion, the Southern Gentleman who is his father can visit them while on business in New York. Connecticut is at once the convenient yet distant site where this white gentleman can situate his colored family and the site of opportunity for his colored son who would have next–to-no opportunity at the South. The Yankee schoolhouse, which we and the ex-colored man enter in the second half of chapter one, complete with all the town's children—black, white, brown—attending school and learning together, exemplifies the opportunities available in the North and unheard of in the South. And so, Johnson's novel begins there, as if to suggest that nothing important did happen, or could happen, before our hero's mother relented and enrolled him at the schoolhouse.

Adults matter in Johnson's schoolhouse episode: the ex-colored man is assigned to "a teacher who knew me;" and we learn this detail: "my mother made her dresses." This hints at a social hierarchy that we are to take into account and strongly suggests that the teacher knows that our racially ambiguous-looking protagonist is colored and has a colored mother. The most interesting detail about the teacher is this: "She was one of the ladies who used to pat me on the head and kiss me."[5] We tend to think of the ex–colored man's amours with white women commencing with the young ladies with whom he later plays duets, just as we assume that whatever Du Bois was up to with white women began with fräuleins in Berlin, not tall newcomers to the Berkshires. But something warm and ardent is present in the way the ex–colored man attaches to his teacher. If nothing more, school is going to be manageable because she is the other mother who has patted him and kissed him. This must be seen in order to comprehend the magnitude of our hero's sense of betrayal when his teacher very publicly "outs" him as a colored child. She, not his real mother, is the mother who does that.

Which brings us to his mother. She is a transplanted southerner who has delayed enrolling her son in the public school apparently in order to put off the day of his inevitable schoolhouse lesson in race. While the effort to protect her son is understandable, the result is that she has raised what we might term a racial misfit. This is suggested when he rattles on about calling the really smart black boy in his class "Shiny," adding idiotically, "to that name he answered good-naturedly during the balance of his public school days" (ECM 9), and it is confirmed when it turns out that he is one of the boys who walks behind the colored children on their way home from school chanting "Nigger, nigger, never die, / Black face and shiny eye" (10). On one occasion, a colored boy turns and hurls his slate, which gashes a white boy, and runs, as do the other colored youths. The ex–colored man then relates, "We ran after them pelting them with stones" (ECM 10). This is, of course, a very revealing "We."

When our hero arrives home that day and tells his mother what occurred, her behavior is as extraordinary as his has been. Furious with her son, she lights into him, saying, " 'Don't you ever use that word [nigger] again . . . and don't you ever bother the colored children at school. You ought to be ashamed of yourself' " (ECM 10). Left out of all of this, most obviously, is the point that he is colored, too, and so is she. One senses that this is but the most recent moment when the mother could have "schooled" her son about his racial identity but has refused to do so. What she doesn't realize is that in avoiding the subject she creates a space in which other ideas and behaviors may take hold.

It is a wonder that it is not until the end of his second term of school that the ex–colored man learns of his race. For whatever reason, the school principal arrives at his classroom and asks "all the white scholars to stand for a moment." This is what happens next: "I [the ex–colored man] rose with the others. The teacher looked at me and, calling my name, said: 'You sit down for the present, and rise with the others.' I did not quite understand her, and questioned: 'Ma'm?' She repeated, with a softer tone in her voice: 'You sit down now, and rise with the others.' I sat down dazed. I saw and heard nothing. When the others were asked to rise, I did not know it. When school was dismissed, I went out in a kind of stupor" (ECM 11).

One thing that conveys this young boy's confusion is the ambiguity of who the "others" are in this scene. He rose with "the others," but then is told (twice) to sit down and rise with "the others." And once "the others" sat down, "the others" rose? Not surprisingly, the boy ends up not standing with either group of others. He is initiated into that particular status as well. His teacher turns out to be the mother who schools him on race, and she is in this scene both instructive and maternal. She is honest, but she speaks softly, and if she seems slightly evasive in her language it is because she cannot help attempting to protect this boy at the same time that she is exposing him, in several senses of the term.

In Du Bois's schoolhouse episode, we have no idea how the others reacted to young Du Bois being rebuffed by the tall newcomer girl. We do not know if they were aware of the incident, or if aware of it, whether they even deemed it racial. In Johnson's novel, the remainder of the episode is carefully designed to display a gamut of reactions to the young ex–colored man's outing. We are told right off that a few of the white boys jeered: " 'Oh, you're a nigger too' " (ECM 11). We don't learn how the white girls reacted, but some of the black children were heard saying, " 'We knew he was colored' " (11). The "We" in that utterance is as conspicuous as "nigger" is in the dialogue attributed to the white boys. The smart black boy whom our young hero unforgivably has called "Shiny" shows that he is already some kind of moral force when he tells the black children, "Come along, don't tease him' " (11). "Red Head," a big slow-witted white boy who is the one other child in this episode with a name (and note that it is also, arguably, a racially descriptive name), walks our young boy home, and additionally expresses his compassion by carrying his friend's books and promising a present the next day. So there are good guys, two of them, one black, one white, one smart, one slow, and so forth. "Two-ness" in this episode is not strictly the "two souls" or "two warring ideals in one dark body" (S 38) that is Du Bois's subject; it is in this instance less spiritual.

As we will also see in Obama's schoolhouse episode, returning home after "that day" at school can be part of the story. Our young boy arrives home and, finding his mother busy with a customer, rushes to his room and to the looking-glass on his wall. Clearly, this is this episode's enactment of "looking at one's self through the eyes of others." Soon, he will also scrutinize his mother's visage in a way he has never done before. What is extraordinary about this moment is that he stands before the mirror searching for race and discovers instead his own beauty. One finds in the literature occasional passages in which a colored man's good looks are almost erotically described; think of Douglass's account of Madison Washington's "heroic" appearance in "The Heroic Slave" or of how Ellison's Invisible Man introduces us to Tod Clifton. But there is nothing, certainly not before 1912, when Johnson's novel appeared, quite like the young ex–colored man's gaze upon himself. Here is the passage:

> I had often heard people say to my mother: "What a pretty boy you have!" I was accustomed to hear remarks about my beauty; but now, for the first time, I became conscious of it and recognized it. I noticed the ivory whiteness of my skin, the beauty of my mouth, the size and liquid darkness of my eyes, and how the long, black lashes that fringed and shaded them produced an effect that was strangely fascinating even to me. I noticed the softness and glossiness of my dark hair that fell in waves over my temples, making my forehead appear whiter than it really was. How long I stood there gazing at my image I do not know. (ECM 11–12)

What we may see here is a child's genuine confusion: he has been informed at school, by his teacher no less, that he is colored, and out on the street he's been called a nigger, but he looks in the mirror and what he's been called is not what he sees. But to push the matter further: what he sees is beauty, white beauty; that is what he recognizes for the first time and what he is "conscious" of. What he sees is not just a white boy but a pretty white boy. No one detail confirms this; they all do. It may be anxiety that is taking over, it may be anger; either way, he's driven to build his case. In psychoanalytic terms, what he seeks is "relief from otherwise unbearable constellations of identification and wishing."[6]

The events of the day have given our young fellow the vocabulary with which to ask his mother some burning questions: "Tell me, mother, am I a nigger?" And after she fumbles with that he asks, "Well, mother, am I white? Are you white?" (ECM 12). These are, of course, questions and issues she has been carefully avoiding, especially in conversations with her son. Thrown off balance, the mother stumbles into another morass: the subject of who our young boy's father is. What she most revealingly manages to say to her son about his father is "the best blood of the South is in you" (12). This declaration may convey the mother's admiration for her child's father, but it also suggests that her thoughts on this difficult subject are bundled up inside timeworn clichés. That is how she manages; that is why the conversation she promises to have with her son "some day" is likely to be unhelpful, if it occurs at all.

All of the protagonists in the schoolhouse episodes under discussion appear in circumstances of remove from one or both parents. Du Bois lived with his mother as a young boy, his father having left them when Du Bois was two, but, as we have seen, there is no parental voice or presence in what he chooses to remember and to present of the visiting-card incident at school.

Johnson's young ex–colored man lives with his mother and, one could say, has another mother in his teacher at school. Learning more about race from his "white mother" than from his colored mother proves to be a feature of his dilemma. His father is present as an absence, as a subject to be broached in the future—not now, never now. In Obama's narrative, young Barack has returned to Hawaii—to America—from Indonesia to live with his grandparents while he matriculates at Punahou Academy. His mother remains in Indonesia; his father, who left the family when Barack was an infant, is far away in his native Kenya. As we will see, Obama's schoolhouse episode turns on the reentry into young Barack's life of both his mother and his father.

In *Their Eyes Were Watching God* (1937), Zora Neale Hurston's Janie Crawford begins the story of her life with this information:

> "Ah ain't never seen mah papa. And Ah didn't know 'im if Ah did. Mah mama neither. She was gone from round dere long before Ah wuz big enough tuh know. Mah grandma raised me. Mah grandma and de white folks she worked wid. She had a house out in de back-yard and dat's where Ah wuz born."[7]

Right off we learn that Janie is virtually an orphan, that she speaks a thick folk speech, and that she and her grandmother reside within a particular proximity to the white people in their lives. As we have seen, the presence or the absence of names is important in these narratives. Janie's grandma is nanny to the white Washburn children and is called "Nanny"; she has no other name. Janie also calls her grandma "Nanny," which is presented as evidence that Janie "was wid dem white chillen so much till Ah didn't know Ah wuzn't white till Ah was round six years old" (T 8).

We have good reason to anticipate that what happened to Janie when she was six was that she entered school and, perhaps on the first day, got a race lesson. But this episode unfolds a bit differently, partly because the setting is the South, not Du Bois's and Johnson's New England, and Janie is destined for a segregated all-black school, not an integrated one. In this instance, discovering one's race is a preparation for school; other lessons await at the schoolhouse.

In Johnson's novel, the young protagonist peers at himself in the mirror; in Hurston's tale, young Janie looks for herself—futilely at first—in a photograph taken of her and the Washburn children, white children who are about to go off to their own segregated school. Janie relates: " 'So when we looked at de picture and everybody got pointed out there wasn't nobody left except a real dark little girl with long hair standing by Eleanor. Dat's where Ah wuz s'posed to be, but Ah couldn't recognize dat dark chile as me. So Ah ast, 'where is me? Ah don't see me' " (T 9). Janie sees a "dark little girl" standing next to a white girl with a proper name and knows, just knows, she isn't "dat dark chile," the lapse into dialect in itself conveying the status she assigns to what she sees and can't "recognize."

Miss Nellie, a white Washburn woman who is a widow and a mother, points to the "dark one" in the picture and says to Janie, using her nickname as term of endearment, " 'Dat's you, Alphabet, don't you know yo' ownself?' " Janie's response is, " 'Aw, aw! I'm colored!' " (T 9). This prompts much hard laughter, from everybody. Miss Nellie is not unlike the teacher in the young ex–colored man's episode: she is the white mother who fills in, somewhat, for the colored mother who is variously missing from action.

The curious nickname with which she addresses Janie is explained by Janie as follows: " 'Dey all useter call me Alphabet 'cause so many people had done named me different names' " (T 9). What's disturbing here is not just that the colored girl has a comic name in contrast to Eleanor, the white girl standing next to her, but that the nickname results from people habitually calling her anything they want to call her. Hurston is as interested as all our authors are in presenting these everyday moments for what they are: scenes of subjection.

Janie's tormentors at school are led by "uh knotty head gal name Mayrella." One of their sports is to taunt Janie about being illegitimate; they especially like the part in the gossip about how her father was hunted down by Mr. Washburn and the sheriff and the hound dogs "for whut he done tuh mah mama" (T 9). Of this, Janie pointedly observes that the children always remembered "de bloodhound part" but not her father's name. While we wonder about all the reasons why Mr. Washburn might be so exercised about catching the man who impregnated Janie's mother, who is, in a sense, a colored member of the family, this is not necessarily a racial incident: bastards and their parents have been berated for time out of mind in every society. What is racial, intraracial, is the grief Janie receives about her dress and her looks. Janie knows she is colored; what awaits her at the schoolhouse is the accusation from black children that she isn't colored enough.

We are told that Mayrella "useter git mad every time she look at me" (T 9). What she sees is Janie's long hair, which has already been remarked upon several times in the novel's early pages. Mayrella is especially frenzied by the bows that adorn Janie's hair, and by the clothes Janie wears that, even as hand-me-downs from the white children, are better than what the black children are wearing. Egged on by Mayrella, the children pick at Janie, push her away from "de ring plays," and tell her "not to be takin' on" over her looks. Janie is colored, she is Nanny's granddaughter, but she is dressed for school and otherwise fussed over by the white Washburn women: this is her twoness, this is what is exposed and problematized in the school setting. Janie does not act privileged (as far as we know), but the spectacle and threat of privilege prompts the black children to taunt and to ostracize her because she lives "in the white folks' back-yard" (T 9). This last thing is the matter Nanny acts upon. Janie tells us: "'Nanny didn't love tuh see me wid mah head hung down, so she figgered it would be mo' better fuh me if we had uh house. So she got the land and everything and then Mis' Washburn helped out a whole heap wid things'" (10). And this is how Nanny acquires the gatepost at which she later spies a teenage Janie kissing Johnny Taylor.

Janie's schoolhouse episode ends with Nanny finding a house for them, perhaps even buying a house for them. One imagines that this no more satisfied the black schoolchildren and their parents than it did the mostly male African American critics (I'm thinking mainly of Sterling Brown, Alain Locke, and Richard Wright) of the late 1930s who criticized Hurston for not presenting the "real problems" before the Negro at the South.[8] Nanny's acquisition of a house, with help from Miss Washburn, likely does nothing to allay the novel's black community's suspicions of Janie's sense of privilege, based in white support. And that may be Hurston's point: black women successfully seeking rooms of their own, in America, achieve something and nothing. Janie may well recall what the black folks said about her Nanny's house when she returns from the muck and hears the folks sniping about her having a house all her own in Eatonville. What she is recalling is part and parcel of what her formative schoolhouse episode first instructed.

In *Dreams from My Father*, ten-year-old Barack Obama's flight to Hawaii to begin classes at Punahou Academy may be characterized as a young boy's return to America for race lessons. Whereas features of the episode border on the unique—Hawaii is not part of the mainland, Punahou is a prestigious private school, Obama lives with his white grandparents, he is African American because his father really is African—the episode as a whole is something of a twice-told tale, an age-old rite of passage.

Preceding the events at school is the remarkable moment of Obama's arrival at the airport in Honolulu and his recollection of how he was overwhelmed by a sense of transition and of two-ness, and how he acted out that two-ness, while searching the crowds for his grandparents. He tells us that he was carrying an Indonesian mask and that he suddenly put it on, took in its "nutty, cinnamon smell," and felt himself "drifting back across oceans and over the clouds, into the violet horizon, back to the place where I had been."[9] But then his name is called and he drops the mask to his side and sees his grandparents. Yet there is more: Obama, "without thinking," returns the mask to his face and performs a little dance for his grandparents, who are amused. This goes on until a customs official taps him on the shoulder and asks him if he is an American. With that, the mask is again lowered.

What a piece of business this is: at very least, we see a biracial child greeting and attempting to please his white elders, using the props at hand, which include the faces of his identity. The masking and unmasking stops with the question about official citizenship; the customs officer wants to see a passport. But it seems as if he is also policing the racial order: put that mask away, he seems to be saying. This is America!

Obama's first day of school begins with Gramps (the grand-father) proudly escorting him to the well-appointed campus, ar-riving early in fact, full of excitement. While it is suggested that Gramps is busy fantasizing about what it would have been like if he had attended such a fancy school, he is also, by plan or na-ture, on a mission: to clarify who his colored grandson is and how he's the boy's grandfather and part of the picture. This is not a schoolhouse episode in which the subject of race is avoided or whispered about. Obama's grandfather walks right up to the teacher and introduces himself. By the time he is done, he has told the teacher, Miss Hefty (the only teacher in this discussion to have a name), that Obama's mother is his daughter and that his father is Kenyan and living in Kenya, and much more. Miss Hefty cannot begin the school day until Gramps has completed his introduction.

Unintentionally, Gramps creates one confusion: he calls Barack "Barry" and introduces Barack to a Chinese boy named Frederick as "Barry." One assumes that Barack is "Barry" to everyone he's met that morning until Miss Hefty calls the roll and the mostly white school children hear a strange name: "Barack Hussein Obama." Immediately, "titters break across the room" (D 59). Miss Hefty hears the titters and attempts to address the situation by asking Barack if he prefers "Barry," while declaring at the same time, "Barack is such a beautiful name." Once again, the names deployed in a schoolhouse episode are telling us much about identities assumed and identities imposed. Barack is Barack, but he is also, especially while a schoolboy, Barry; even his Kenyan father, who is named Barack, calls him Barry. This is a lot for a ten-year-old to process and to put in place.

Miss Hefty reminds us of the teacher in the ex–colored man's episode: she is kind, she has personal reasons for feeling attached to her colored pupil (Miss Hefty has lived in Kenya), and she doesn't seem to be aware of the pain she is causing when she "outs" Barack. What the ex–colored man calls his teacher's "swordthrust" comes in Obama's first-day episode when Miss Hefty asks young Barack, "Do you know what tribe your father is from?" (D 60). He is speechless. Being asked, in effect, to other yourself in front of strangers who have already laughed at your name is unbearable. When he finally answers, he says, "Luo." Miss Hefty's question does not create respect for Barack, the new boy; to the contrary, "a sandy-haired boy . . . repeated

the word [Luo] in a loud hoot, like the sound of a monkey"
(60), and pandemonium breaks out in the classroom. Apparently, even at a young age, these children know intuitively that
racism's project is to primitivize the other; in this scene, monkey
sounds do that work (H xvii).

The sandy-haired boy, like Du Bois's tall newcomer, gets no
other name. It is not so much that he doesn't "deserve" a name
in the narrative but that he is a specter in a memory that is painful to assemble. He is not the only such figure Barack encounters in the "daze" of the rest of the school day. There is the
"red-headed girl" who wanted to touch his hair and "seemed
hurt" when he refused. And there is the "ruddy-faced boy" who
asked if Barack's father ate people. Once again, names are not
offered because this is not, in truth, individualized, idiosyncratic
behavior. These children represent a shared mindset, an igno-
rance that is at best a part of their innocence.

The first day of school begins with the grandfather and ends
with him as well. As he merrily prepares dinner, he asks, " 'So
how was it? Isn't it terrific that Miss Hefty used to live in Kenya?
Makes the first day a little easier, I'll bet' " (D 60). Well, actually,
it did not make the first day easier. But she has good intentions;
Gramps has good intentions. Good intentions abound. But
good intentions did not prevent the day of school Barack just
endured. Little wonder, then, that in a sentence starkly centered
on the page, in a paragraph unto itself, Obama next writes: "I
went into my room and closed the door" (60).

The schoolmate who does have a name is Coretta. She is
"plump and dark" and the one other black child in Obama's
class. Before his arrival, she has been the only black student in
their grade. Just as we cannot help being alert to the fact that
she is named, we cannot help but wonder at the name bestowed
on her. If indeed, Obama changed the names of most of the
persons in his narrative (D xvii), what alchemy, what civil-rights-

laden, historical gesture, led him to name this particular black girl "Coretta"? Young Barack and Coretta avoid each other but watch each other, as if to gain lessons on how to deal with their classroom situation without doing something as obvious and "tribal" as openly conversing and being friends. But there comes a day, a "hot, cloudless day," when Barack and Coretta spontaneously begin to play with each other during recess, and in the midst of chasing each other, fall to the ground, "breathless." When Barack looks up, he discovers to his horror that he and Coretta are surrounded by white classmates screaming, "Coretta has a boyfriend!" (61).

Perhaps especially for preadolescents, any innocent episode with unwanted sexual implications is devastating. But this moment is exheedingly unbearable for young Barack because the equation includes race as well as sex. Barack is down on the ground not just with any girl but with the black girl, and the taunts from the white children carry the suggestion that he and the black girl are out on the playground doing what black people do, when given the chance. No wonder, then, that Barack screams back that he is *not* Coretta's boyfriend, and gives her a shove, to boot.

Among the key features of this schoolhouse scene is the fact that Obama's memory recalls that Coretta chased him; it was not the other way around. This suggests Obama's conviction, as an adult, that this episode, or one similar to it, was bound to happen—bound to catch up with him. It is also notable that the taunting white children are on high, pointing down at Barack and Coretta, assuming, as it were, a hierarchical position at the same time that they are "faceless." Earlier in *Dreams,* the offending children have sandy hair or red hair or a ruddy face; these children on the playground are faceless and even more specter-like. Most extraordinary in the scene is Obama's acute awareness of how in pushing Coretta away and yelling "leave me alone!" he was also letting her down. This is, in his words, his "betrayal" of Coretta. Just as Du Bois will never forget the glance of the tall newcomer girl, Obama will forever recall the look on Coretta's face after he pushed her. He tells us that the look brimmed with "disappointment" and "accusation" (D 61). And he admits that "somehow I'd been tested and found wanting" (61). But there are lessons in failures: the episode with Coretta schools Obama to seek the "true self-consciousness" (Du Bois's term) that hopefully disappoints no one, including one's self.

A telegram arrives, and suddenly Barack and his grandparents are nervously aware that Barack's father is coming from Kenya to see him and is staying through the Christmas holidays. Barack's mother is soon arriving in Hawaii as well, two weeks before his father, but the consternation is not about her, it is about Barack Senior. The thought of him is what creates a "moment the air was sucked out of the room" (62) and what later prompts Gramps to say, " 'Should be one hell of a Christmas' " (D 63).

During the weeks Barack and his mother have together before Barack Senior arrives, she "stuffs" Barack with information about Kenya and its history. One might think that a bit of schooling on Kenya would abate the confusion enveloping both Barack and his mother, but it doesn't work. He writes, "But nothing my mother told me could relieve my doubts, and I retained little of the information she offered" (D 64). Part of the problem is that young Barack wants stories, myths even, and images, not facts. His own attempts to find or create those stories are unsuccessful and rather self-incriminating. But Obama nonetheless carries on with this aspect of the story so that we might see how a boy attempts to contend not so much with the familiar matter of his father's absence but with the new dilemma of his pending return.

School is the venue for one key scene of story creation. Another child might have dealt with the confusion of having a mysterious parent arriving from another part of the world by being secretive about the whole matter. Not so our young Barack. He's voluble on the subject; he's got stories, including the inevitable tale some anxious black children try to tell about how, back in the motherland, "my father was a prince" (D 63). The boys at his lunch table get interested, and that's an added bonus: Barack is negotiating his status at the schoolhouse as well as his personal befuddlement. One of the boys has a question, "I mean, will you go back and be a prince?" Barack replies, "'Well . . . if I want to, I could. It's sort of complicated, see, 'cause the tribe is full is warriors'" (63). It sure is complicated, and not just because of the warriors! It's complicated because Barack is attempting to make whole cloth out of remnants, "the scraps of information I'd picked up from my mother" (63). He trying to find the useable story, the story that meets needs and that can be altered "on a whim" or ignored "when convenient" (63). He seeks the story he can depend on because he already knows it is too risky to depend on his father.

Barack Senior arrives, and Barack is let out of school early that day by Miss Hefty, who wishes him good luck. This occasions the second long walk home from school in the chapter, the first having been the trudge home after the humiliations of the first day of school. Obama describes the walk home in these terms: "I left the school building feeling like a condemned man. My legs were heavy, and with each approaching step toward my grandparents' apartment, the thump in my chest grew louder. When I entered the elevator, I stood without pressing the button" (D 64). In this instance, what makes the walk home excruciating is not something that happened at school but what awaits him at home, his father, the stranger.

When Barack's grandmother opens the door and says, " 'Come on, Bar . . . come meet your father' " (D 65), we realize that he may well be *meeting* his father. What is there for him to remember of the man? Perhaps to amend the grandmother's use of the word "meet," Barack Senior stresses that "It is a good thing to see you after so long" (65), and he addresses his son as "Barry." Calling him "Barry" is an act of affection meant to put young Barack at ease; it also a familial gesture, a way of saying I, too, am of the family that calls you Barry. But when Barack Senior calls Barack "Barry," he is also calling attention to the fact that Barack is his American son, his son from his (first?) marriage to an American woman. When Barack's father calls him "Barry" there is another lesson in two-ness in that.

School is a subject or an issue throughout the family's strange month together. Barack Senior immediately asks young Barack about school in their first conversation, letting him know that he's already heard about how well Barack is doing in his studies. This seems at first to be idle, conventional talk, but he is actually pursing an important concern: he is initiating friendship with his son while proclaiming him an Obama. At one point, he says, "Have I told you that your brothers and sister have also excelled in their schooling? It's in the blood, I think" (D 65). Of course, this is a way of underscoring for his son an important thing he wants him to know about himself: that he was a good student and is a studious man. There is risk in this: every adult in that small living room knows that he left his family rather than pass up graduate school at Harvard. But at the beginning of the month together, on the first day in fact, everyone is on good behavior.

Weeks into the visit, however, resentments burn, and tempers begin to flare. The eruption Obama reports occurs one evening just before the Christmas recess at school. Barack turns on the television to watch *How the Grinch Stole Christmas,* and his father summarily orders him to turn it off and to go to his room and study, so the adults can talk. Toot (the grandmother) suggests that Barack watch the show in the bedroom; his father says no. Barack's mother tries to explain that it's almost Christmas and that the cartoon is a Christmas favorite and that Barry's been looking forward to it all week. His father says, " 'Anna, this is nonsense. If the boy has done his work for tomorrow, he can begin on his next day's assignments. Or the assignments he will have when he returns from the holidays' " (D 68). And he has more words for his son: " 'I tell you, Barry, you do not work as hard as you should. Go now, before I get angry at you' " (68). With that, all hell breaks loose; everybody's yelling and furious. The scene turns from How the Grinch Stole Christmas to how the Father stole Christmas. While the ensuing argument was inevitable, and could have been about almost anything, it is revealing that Barack Senior makes it an argument about school. This is another school matter from which Barack retreats to his room.

The next day, his mother has some news for him: " 'By the way, I forgot to tell you that Miss Hefty has invited your father to come to school on Thursday. She wants him to speak to the class' " (D 69). His response is: "I couldn't imagine worse news. I spent that night and all of the next day trying to suppress thoughts of the inevitable: the faces of my classmates when they heard about mud huts, all my lies exposed, the painful jokes afterward" (69). Clearly, with the mention of the classmates' faces, we have in Obama's reaction another phrasing of double-consciousness, of "looking at one's self through the eyes of others" (S 38). This is a feature of our other narratives; consider Du Bois remembering the glance of the newcomer girl or Hurston's Janie unhinged by the looks from Mayrella. What may be singular about Obama's circumstance is that the faces of his classmates include Coretta's face; what will be her look this time?

What also may be unique is that Barack's anxieties about how the children will look at him are totally bound up with how they will see his father. What will they see?

What they see is a highly educated man from Kenya who has been introducing his country, and himself, to myriad audiences for a good long while. Barack Senior is especially deft at speaking to an American audience: Africa is in his narrative, but so is America. And so, while there are wild animals and tribal customs in what he describes, there is also a surprisingly familiar story of a country's struggle for freedom from British colonial rule. This is what Obama remembers of that part of the speech: "And he told us of Kenya's struggle to be free, how the British wanted to stay and unjustly rule the people, just as they had in America; how many had been enslaved only because of the color of their skin, just as they had in America; but that Kenyans, like all of us in the room, longed to be free and develop themselves through hard work and sacrifice" (D 70).

Barack's father's speech at the school is a lesson in inclusiveness, in what is shared. *Dreams from My Father* offers the rare schoolhouse episode in which the parent actually comes to school, and everyone, including the child who dreaded the parent's appearance, is the better for it. The schoolhouse scenes in *Dreams* begin with Gramps coming to school and end with Barack Senior coming to school; this is typical of the kind of symmetry Obama often constructs in telling his stories. Symmetry is additionally offered when classmates who appeared in the early scenes reappear right after his father's address. For example, the ruddy-faced boy who on the first school day asked if Barack's father eats people comes up to Barack to say, " 'Your dad is pretty cool' " (D 70). In a more complicated way, Coretta is part of the moment as well. As before, she does not speak; she says nothing to Barack or to his father. Off to the side, she watches his father say goodbye to some of the children. Since she and Barack are the only colored children in the class, this means, of course, that she is watching Barack's father say goodbye to white children. What is she looking for? What does she see? Obama tells us that "her face showed only a simple satisfaction" (70). What does that mean?

Barack Senior's arrival and departure are marked with gifts to his son. The evening of his arrival, he gives Barack three wooden figurines: "a lion, an elephant, and an ebony man in tribal dress beating a drum" (D 66). Barack doesn't know what to say, perhaps because gifts from his father are so rare, or perhaps because these figures represent the very sort of images of Africa that prompt children like his classmates to giggle and crack jokes. His mother urges him to say thank you; Barack mutters his thanks. The figurines are described as being "lifeless in his hands" (66). The question is thus raised as to whether the figurines, and the father who bestowed them, will, in some measure, come to life for Barack. Will they and the father become something more than curios from a dark place far away?

Barack Senior comes to life, at least for a golden moment, when he gives departing gifts to his son. The gifts are records, 45s, which he gives to Barack, saying, "'Barry! Look here—I forgot that I brought these for you. The sounds of your continent'" (D 71). The records bring the continent alive as the figurines never could because the music begins and Barack's father begins to dance. Though still hobbled from his automobile accident, the man knows his steps and can move. And then he does a wonderful thing: he invites Barack to join him in the dance. His very words are "Come, Barry, . . . you will learn from the master'" (71). As they dance, Barack watches his father tingle with life and with pleasure, his eyes closed, his whole self transported. But suddenly he opens one eye and peeks at his son and grins a silly grin; he's keeping track of his boy; he's schooling him in something indescribable. Obama remembers it this way: "I took my first tentative steps with my eyes closed, down, up, my arms swinging, the voices lifting . . . And I hear him still . . . I follow my father into the sound" (71).

Barack's grandfather was right in his prediction: especially with Barack Senior around, it was going to be one hell of a Christmas. Barack Senior came to town, came to school, in fact. In the photos Obama has of that visit (the only photos he has of himself with his father), he and his father stand before the Christmas tree, his father sporting the tie he has just received as a gift from Barack. Barack is next to his father, holding an orange basketball, his father's gift to him. These are the "official" Christmas gifts, the ones recorded in photographs, the ones with no strings attached. But other gifts, wanted and unwanted, were no doubt exchanged—the figurines and records, yes, but others, too; some tangible, some ephemeral, some known to be gifts only with the passage of time. We learn from the giving and receiving of gifts, and this can be a part of our schooling, as we know from reading the schoolhouse episodes in African American narratives. Obama learned much during his first months of American schooling, thanks in part to the gifts and dreams from his father.

TONI MORRISON, BARACK OBAMA, AND DIFFERENCE

> Sotto (but not completely) is my own giggle (in Afro-American terms) of the proto-myth of the journey to manhood. Whenever characters are cloaked in Western fable, they are in deep trouble; but the African myth is also contaminated.
>
> —Toni Morrison

> I know that the hardening of lines, the embrace of fundamentalism and tribe, dooms us all.
>
> —Barack Obama

In this lecture series on reading the African American classics in the age of Obama, we are discussing themes and tropes that are not new (indeed, they are "classic") but that are received anew because we have been reading and listening to Barack Obama's personal narratives, and because we have been observing him living out and, in a sense, performing his narratives often on a very public stage.[1] For example, narratives of the absent parent, and of the black father who has absconded, are in truth twice-told tales, but we read or receive those tales in new ways in the present moment because our president has shared with us his own versions of those stories. Indeed, with African American folklore and Toni Morrison's *Song of Solomon* (1977) in mind, we can even say (with a bit of blues intonation) that Mr. Obama knows all about Africans flying off to Africa, leaving children who must try to find family and home in new arrangements and, often, new geographies.[2]

Absent parents abound in the narratives under discussion, and in the case of most of our narratives, including Frederick Douglass's autobiography and Zora Neale Hurston's story of Janie Crawford, the fathers were never present. Raising yourself under these sorts of circumstances, perhaps with the additional pressure of raising yourself to be a black man or woman with few models of that kind of self-fashioning before you, has been a concern in many of our narratives as well. As we have seen, Barack Obama speaks for many black male protagonists of any era when he declares in the early pages of *Dreams from My Father* (1995): "I was trying to raise myself to be a black man in America, and beyond the given of my appearance, no one around me seemed to know exactly what that meant" (D 76). Generally speaking, all of our figures are negotiating the myriad forms and pressures of two-ness in their lives. "Two-ness" obviously includes the sensation of seeing one's self through the eyes of others that Dr. Du Bois so famously termed the Negro's "double-consciousness." But two-ness is so many things: the forging of a biracial identity, for example, or facing the decision to choose between a biracial identity and a racial identity. Two-ness for Hurston's Janie Crawford is, as it often may be for girls and women, a matter of adornment: she is black but adorned with flowing long hair; she is black but she lives with her grandmother "in the white folks' backyard," as her schoolmates put it, and the white women dress her and grace her hair with bows. Two-ness for Morrison's Milkman Dead takes many forms, including, as we will discuss, two mothers in Ruth and Pilate, and two versions, one from his father Macon and one from his mother Ruth, of what his father calls the "whole truth" of their marriage. The marriage is both intact and nonexistent; Milkman lives with his parents but, in a real sense, has been abandoned by them. Milkman is another of our characters who is fitfully "finding the personality to deal with the pain of abandonment."[3]

In his narratives, Frederick Douglass tells us that even as a boy, even before he knew the days of the week or the months of the year, he knew that he would have to find a home elsewhere. In *My Bondage and My Freedom* (1855) especially, he describes his efforts in Baltimore, and later on the Freeland plantation, to create Sabbath schools and to foster caring and community among black people. Douglass was negotiating being variously abandoned in the world by creating community and by creating a communal self as well. He was, in short, a community organizer, organizing community and self, and we see this with a special clarity today because of Barack Obama's narratives of community organizing, which are also, rather clearly, narratives of self-invention. In Morrison's *Song of Solomon*, Milkman's inabilities to create himself involve, in great part, his inability to imagine a self that is of a community and communal. Morrison can imagine a character of Milkman's deficiencies precisely because she is invested in her own commitment to "organizing" communities in her art.[4]

The community Morrison organizes in *Song of Solomon* is a Great Migration neighborhood. While certain details indicate that this is a black neighborhood up north in a Michigan city, quite possibly Detroit as some have guessed, Morrison is deliberately not specific, allowing us to imagine that the "Southside" in her story could be any of a number of southsides created by the Negro migrations, including the southsides we readers may have lived in. With the telling exception of Ruth Foster and her children—Magdalena, First Corinthians, and Milkman—most every character is a recent migrant from the South: Guitar Bains and his grandmother are from Florida; Macon and Pilate Dead arrive from Pennsylvania but are southern people with roots in Virginia and ties to Georgia; the various unnamed black folk living on "Not Doctor Street" are specifically described as being from Louisiana, Alabama, Georgia, and Virginia. More often than not, these migrants are survivors, people who in general somehow survived the punishments of black southern living, but also people who are specifically the survivors of trauma: Macon and Pilate saw their daddy (the "Pennsylvania African," as Macon likes to remember him) blown off a fence by gunfire; Guitar remembers when his father was sawn in two at the mill, lengthwise. The darker story of the great Negro migrations is that some people who migrated, who sought a home elsewhere, were people left behind. They were abandoned people, and it is their stories that get told in Morrison's novel.

The black southside in Morrison's story is not monolithic; it is, as Wendy Harding and Jacky Martin would describe it, a Morrisonian "world of difference."[5] Difference is most overtly seen in observing the obvious haves and have nots, the haves being the Macon Dead family, replete with properties, a Packard automobile, and summer sojourns on Honore Island, and the have nots being everyone else. Indeed, it could be said that the neighborhood is peopled by the Deads, and by the tenants of the Deads. But that does not account for Pilate and her household, and it is with Pilate's presence that we see how Morrison is once again, deliberately, complicating difference. Ostensibly, Pilate and daughter Reba and granddaughter Hagar are have nots: they don't have electricity or gas or much of anything else. But there is a difference between not having electricity because you can't afford it and not having electricity because you don't want to pay for it. Pilate, Reba, and Hagar make wine, sell it, and make money, but not to pay for utility bills.

These women also sing together, and make an irresistible music. At the end of chapter 1, Macon Dead takes a shortcut home that leads him past Pilate's house. He hurries along but then hears the women singing:

> He turned back and walked slowly toward Pilate's house. They were singing some melody that Pilate was leading. A phrase that

the other two were taking up and building on. . . . Surrendering
to the sound, Macon moved closer. . . . Near the window, hidden by the dark, he felt the irritability of the day drain from him
and relished the effortless beauty of the women singing in the
candlelight.[6]

Macon admits at one point that he is drawn to the music because he knows no music awaits him at his own home. What
Pilate and the women have, and makes them haves in the story,
is collectivity, albeit a fragile collectivity. They represent, especially in their singing, a powerful rendering of what Harding
and Martin call the "community chorus" (W 90) in *Song of Solomon*. In Morrison's novels, the singing, storytelling, and joking, as well as the nourishing and healing, are all activities that
seek to form collectivity or to maintain it. And we note, of
course, that the people pursuing these essential ways of being
alive, no matter whether at the barber shop or general store or
at Pilate's table, are the so-called have nots of the neighborhood.

And so there are two Dead households in the neighborhood,
one headed by Macon, the other led by his sister, Pilate, and
both are wealthy, though in strikingly different terms. Some
readers might want to insist that, in the end, Pilate's household
is much "better off" than Macon's. But it is indeed at the end
that we are confronted with Pilate's death, in addition to
Hagar's. When Pilate whispers to Milkman, "Watch Reba for
me," then dies, we shudder at the thought of Reba being the
survivor, *and* at the thought of Milkman surviving to care for
her. Perhaps that is yet another reason for Milkman to make his
leap at the very end: facing Reba, after "bringing on," so to
speak, the deaths of Hagar and Pilate, is unbearable. That is not
a reason to survive; that is not what African American survival
should entail.

Pilate is Milkman's parent, his mother, who dies violently. She initiates him, as a survivor, into survivor's kinship with herself and her brother, his father, Macon, who both also saw a parent blown away. Moreover, Milkman is now also related to Reba as never before: they are the latest generation of Dead children left behind.

Milkman's actual, biological mother, Ruth Foster Dead, is still alive and there for Milkman, but that is no more a compensation for him than that of his father being alive. Morrison at one point describes Pilate and Ruth as being profoundly similar, noting, "Both were vitally interested in Macon Dead's son, and both had close and supportive post-humous communication with their fathers" (SS 139). But in those details lie differences as well, and the differences have much to do with the self each woman has created as a survivor. Each woman has her own way of being alone in the world. Ruth aptly describes herself as a "small woman"; she is small even in her one aggressive act of conjuring (with Pilate's help) Macon into having sex with her and conceiving Milkman. She is small in this because conceiving is not about family or love, and certainly not about the future of the race, it is about what she will do strictly for herself to mourn her father and to fashion herself a survivor, in her father's house no less.

How she nurtures is telling in this regard. One of the first things we learn about Ruth is that she can't cook—she can't nourish and nurture very well in that regard, perhaps deliberately so—but that she is attentive to going off quietly to what had been her father's study to nurse Milkman at her breast, perhaps even until he is school age. This is how Milkman gets his name: handy man Freddie sees through the window a big boy in Ruth's lap, working away inside her blouse, and that boy is forever known as "Milkman." Macon eventually hears the schoolchildren calling his son "Milkman," and he doesn't like it; to him it sounds "dirty, intimate, and hot" (SS 15). It may not be all that, but it is something Ruth can do to avenge the sexual deprivation forced on her in her marriage since she was twenty.

Ruth's manner of surviving is at best to be self-centered, at worst self-absorbed. She is offended when she discovers that Hagar is trying to kill Milkman and Milkman hasn't said a word about this to her, but what kind of relationship between them is in place that would lead him to confide in her? While her lessons are not explicit, they have taught Milkman to stay with her in her father's house, work for his father, sleep with his cousin (a version of keeping sex within the family), and, in a specifically self-centered way, be small. Ruth's conversations with Pilate, and her insistence on funeral money from Macon for Hagar's service gesture in the direction of collectivity, but she is not of the "community chorus." Indeed, when Macon thinks about how no music is awaiting him at home, the image that leaps before him offers "his wife's unyielding back; his daughters, boiled dry from years of yearning; his son, to whom he could speak only if his words held some command or criticism" (SS 28). This is the home he built, and that Ruth built, too.

Pilate's mode of surviving is to seek out collectives in which to be one within many, or at least, one among several. We see this in her being drawn to the groups of migrant farmworkers with whom she first lives after her father dies, and after she and her brother Macon have quarreled and split up. But Pilate's circumstance cautions that collectives may shun you (the farmworkers send her away or abandon her once they learn that she has no navel; and she has no real community in the black migration neighborhood other than her household), and families may not form (Pilate has a child but is as mate-deprived as Ruth; and the family she hoped to provide for Hagar in moving to Macon Dead's city is something to overcome, not join). Pilate's situation tells us is that the "community chorus" may not form, or may be too fragile to form and last, if the community isn't bigger than yourself or you and the precious few in your midst. Pilate and Reba and Hagar are a chorus unto themselves but are merely an eccentric trio within the community as a whole. Hagar, the youngest, will not pass on what the women know about shared survival; indeed, she is the first to die.

In the singing, Pilate is the leader. This is true at the beginning when Macon hides in the shadows of Darling Street, listening to the women sing, and it is true at the end when, at Hagar's funeral, Pilate begins her chant of "Mercy" and Reba, in a sweet soprano, responds from the other end of the church, singing, "I hear you!" (SS 318). This is in keeping with Pilate being tall, tall among men as well as women, except when she mysteriously shrinks in size while she performs the lie that gets Milkman and Guitar out of jail after they robbed her of her sack of bones. (She reverts to her true height immediately after leaving the police station.) This is also in keeping with Pilate being an independent businesswoman pursuing her own model of individualism within a shared self-sufficiency. People in Southside have opinions about Pilate, but never does someone say of her what Mrs. Bains said of Macon Dead: "A nigger in business is a terrible thing to see" (22). This is because Pilate nurtures; even her winemaking seems of a piece with her preparing the perfect boiled egg for Milkman and Guitar or offering to Ruth a ripe peach.

The most important thing Pilate represents in the novel, and it is related to her best moments of mothering, is a communal self that is woman-made. A comparison of Pilate's self and household to what evolves for Guitar and the Seven Days helps make this point.

At the beginning of *Song of Solomon,* we observe two communal collectives: the household created by Pilate, Reba, and Hagar and the barbershop community that includes Railroad Tommy, Hospital Tommy, Empire State, Nero Brown, a man named Porter who is drunk and pissing and waving a shotgun in the first scene, and the young Guitar. Both of these collectives can be and are communal choruses: this is obviously so when Pilate, Reba, and Hagar sing their special harmonies, and when the brothers at the barbershop get into their high mode of joking and storytelling. But all the men just cited have another way of being a collective, for as we discover in chapter 9, they are members of the Seven Days, an organization that Guitar describes to Milkman in this way:

> "There is a society. It's made up of a few men who are willing to take some risks. They don't initiate anything; they don't even choose. They are as indifferent as rain. But when a Negro child, a Negro woman, or Negro man is killed by whites and nothing is done about it by their law and their courts, this society selects a similar victim at random, and they execute him or her in a similar manner if they can. If a Negro was hanged, they hang; if a Negro was burnt, they burn; raped and murdered, they rape and murder. If they can. If they can't do it precisely in the same manner, they do it any way they can, but they do it. They call themselves the Seven Days. They are made up of seven men." (SS 154–155)

When Guitar is done explaining, Milkman is described as feeling "tight, shriveled, and cold" (155). Milkman asks, " 'Why don't you just hunt down the ones that did the killing? Why kill innocent people? Why not just those who did it?" Guitar replies, "It doesn't matter who did it. Each and every one of them could do it. So you just get any one of them" (155). As the argument stretches on, Guitar says that, as a member of the Seven Days, he cannot marry or have children, but that life is very satisfying because what he's doing is about loving black people (159).

The Seven Days may be a collective, but whether it is communal and loving and nurturing of black people is another matter. It is secretive and, in that sense, withdrawn from the community because, as Guitar says, the community may betray us. There is even a question as to whether it is nurturing of its own members, for, as we learn, Robert Smith, the black insurance man who donned blue wings and leaped to his death in snow scattered with red velvet rose petals (thus completing his red, white, and blue suicide), was a Day. The Seven Days are a collective in what Barack Obama might call their "embrace of fundamentalism and tribe" (D xi), but each member is on his own on his day. There is no chorus. Guitar is on his own in the last pages of the novel, hunting down Milkman, hunting down the gold that will support the Seven Days and sustain the killing. In the last scene of the novel, Milkman is out on the ledge with Pilate, the communal black woman, burying the bones of the ancestral dead, when she is shot dead by Guitar, the communal black man, the Sabbath Day man of the Seven Days. The triangulation of sounds in this catastophe is extraordinary: Guitar raises his rifle and we get the report of his gun; Pilate is too wounded to raise a song but asks Milkman to try; Milkman has never been able to sing, but, as Morrison puts it, he can speak the words "without the least bit of a tune" of a song his womenfolk have taught him. He has heard the communal chorus. And so we ask, given the extent to which Guitar may feel jilted by Milkman, as a friend and as a man, was the killing of Pilate really a shot gone astray?

The first epigraph for this lecture, taken from Toni Morrison's extraordinary essay "Unspeakable Things Unspoken: The Afro-American Presence in American Literature," is from the section of the essay that discusses the first sentence of *Song of Solomon*. Part of that passage reads as follows: "Whenever characters are cloaked in Western fable, they are in deep trouble; but the African myth is also contaminated." I will use that provocative statement as a guide for my remarks in this section of the talk.

There is good reason to believe that "Western fable" in Morrison's remarks refers to is the "male adventure story, the Ulysses theme," and I join the critics who are amused by the blues humor of who Circe is in *Song of Solomon* (an "ancient survivor," almost a specter, not a hottie) and of who is there at the end of the quest instead of Penelope (a dead Hagar and an angry Pilate, who cracks a wine bottle on Milkman's head and throws him down into her basement) (W 72). But I would like to comment on what I'd like to call the acquisition fables in the novel, which are surely "Western," given that capitalism, consumerism, and territorial expansion are indubitably Western.

Macon Dead's story is obviously an acquisition fable. His response to his father's murder and loss of everything, including the gorgeous farm ironically named "Lincoln's Heaven," is to own things, lots of them. Macon is the landlord in our novel. Almost everybody on Southside seems to be a tenant of Macon, including members of the Seven Days. When Porter has his drunken tirade, Macon responds not with concern for the community but with an urgency to collect the rent from Porter before he is arrested or kills himself. When Mrs. Bains, Guitar's grandmother, pleads for more time to pay her rent, urging him to consider all the babies her daughter left her with, Macon says, " 'Can they make it in the street, Mrs. Bains? That's where they gonna be if you don't figure out some way to get me my money.' " This is the episode in which she says, to the children awaiting her, " 'A nigger in business is a terrible thing to see' " (SS 21–22). Macon has acquired lots of houses. He has a key to each one, and the keys comprise a huge ring of keys. Each key is an emblem of his power, but as commentators have noted (W 73), if you liken Macon's collection of keys to an accumulation of tiny phalluses, you have a measure of the man and of his ambitions.

This isn't to say that Macon doesn't dream. At one point, he expounds on his dream of acquiring lakefront properties and being in at the beginning of developing a summer resort for prosperous Negroes. At another point, he describes a land deal he couldn't quite pull off that would have made him the owner of land the Lackawanna Railroad would later need to buy. When word of this gets back to Danville, Pennsylvania, where Macon and Pilate grew up, Macon enters local folklore as the black man who almost bought a railroad. But becoming a story told by the black community chorus in the town where his father was murdered is as big Macon gets, and as close as he comes to having a community. Throughout the novel, Macon is stuck in a barren life as the patriarch of the one intact traditional family in the historical present of the story. He has acquired stuff, including a wife with money and light-skinned daughters, and a son he didn't want but to whom he can leave things, as his father could not do for him. But, in truth, he has nothing.

Acquisition fables are part of the story lived out by the youngest characters, Milkman, Hagar, and Guitar. Milkman's story is mainly one of living fitfully in the world of acquisitions into which he is born. The only house he ever lives in is the elegant residence his mother inherited from her father, the doctor, and which Macon was no doubt happy at first to acquire. The only job he has is in his father's business, and that gives him ready access to the money collected from Macon's tenants. When Milkman decides, at the age of thirty-one, to break off his affair with Hagar, who he has been sleeping with since he was seventeen, he thinks he can make it right if he sends a letter and encloses a nice piece of cash. When Milkman journeys south to Virginia, he packs a big suitcase full of expensive clothes and tucks $500 in his pocket. He gets in a knife fight in the general store not just because he's flashing city clothes and talking about the pretty women (some of whom are no doubt related to the men listening to him) but because he says something offhand about how his car broke down and he just might need to buy another one! That kind of talk incenses people—men—who have little or nothing.

A key moment when Milkman muses on acquiring something he does not already have is when he tells Guitar about Pilate's hanging sack, which she calls her inheritance, and proposes that they steal it, since it surely must contain the gold Macon told him about. The two men scheme a bit and then lapse into fantasies about what they could do with the money. Milkman's thoughts go this way:

> New people. New Places. Command. That's what he wanted in his life. And he couldn't get deep into Guitar's talk of elegant clothes for himself and his brother, sumptuous meals for Uncle Billy, and week-long card games in which the stakes would be a yard and a half and then a deuce and a quarter. He screamed and shouted "Wooeeeee!" at Guitar's list, but because his life was not unpleasant and even had a certain amount of luxury in addition to its comfort, he felt off center. He just wanted to beat a path away from his parents' past, which was also their present and which was threatening to become his present as well. (SS 180)

The problem for Milkman is that the path *away* has to become, at some point, the path *to* something, and as he himself says, he cannot "visualize a life much different from the one he had" (179–180). What he needs to acquire is more than gold; he needs to acquire a self, a life.

Hagar is "thirty-six and nervous" when she gets Milkman's outrageous letter, which he signed "with love, of course, but more than that, with gratitude" (SS 99). Her anger becomes a rage, especially after she sees him in a bar with his arm wrapped around a woman with grey eyes and copper hair, who she hoped was one of his sisters, but, of course, was not. Hagar then stalks

Milkman for six months, trying to kill him whenever there is a full moon. She finds him finally, on one of those moonlit evenings, in Guitar's rented room. She has an ice pick, and she raises it, but she cannot kill him. For a long time, once home, she doesn't speak. Pilate and Reba respond to the situation by cooking special things for her, and by acquiring little presents for her. Little presents for Hagar: that was one thing Pilate and Reba would spend money on; they'd been doing that ever since she was a child. At one point in this acquisition fable, Pilate presents Hagar with a compact "trimmed in a goldlike metal" (309). Hagar opens the compact and stares in the mirror and finally speaks. " 'No wonder,' she said at last. 'Look at that. No wonder. No wonder' " (308).

Determined to fix herself up for her man-boy, Hagar hastily bathes and readies for some serious shopping. Pilate and Reba collude in this by hocking Reba's diamond ring. Having acquired $275 (in exchange for the ring worth $2,000), Hagar shops. Morrison meticulously catalogs for us all of Hagar's purchases, offering items *and* their labels, the effect being that we witness both maniacal shopping and rampant consumerism: "She bought a Playtex garter belt, I. Miller No Color hose, Fruit of the Loom panties, and two nylon slips—one white, one pink—one pair of Joyce Fancy Free and one of Con Brio ('Thank heaven for little Joyce Heels')" (SS 310). After adding in an "Evan-Picone two-piece number" and a white blouse and a nightgown ("fawn trimmed in sea foam" (311)), Hagar shops for makeup. With that turn of event, Hagar's Western fable of accumulation reminds us that she has consumed a certain standard of what is beautiful, and that that drives her shopping, as well as her certainty that this is what is needed to recaptivate Milkman.

On her way home, Hagar gets caught in a driving rainstorm, and her new possessions are ruined:

She was thoroughly soaked before she realized it was raining and then only because one of the shopping bags split. When she looked down, her Evan-Picone white-with-band-of-color skirt was lying in a neat half fold on the shoulder of the road. . . . She pulled out the box of Con Brios, a smaller package of Van Raalte gloves, and another containing her fawn-trimmed-in-sea-foam shortie nightgown. These she stuffed into the other bag. Retracing her steps, she found herself unable to carry the heavier bag in one hand, so she hoisted it up to her stomach and hugged it with both arms. She had hardly gone ten yards when the bottom fell out of it. (SS 313)

What happens next is that Hagar begins to trip over the cosmetics, with names like "Jungle Red" and "Youth Blend" and "Sunny Glow," scents and passions she'd hoped to acquire.

She finally gets home with her damaged goods, hurriedly dresses and primps, and presents herself to Pilate and Reba. Their stricken eyes direct her to see what she hadn't seen in the mirror: "the wet hose, the soiled white dress, the sticky, lumpy, face powder, the streaked rouge, and the wet, wild shoals of hair" (SS 314). With this final catalogue, Morrison brilliantly concludes this acquisition fable, reminding us that losses accumulate, too. There is another sad conversation in which Hagar raves about what Milkman wants a woman to look like: she is still reliving seeing him in that bar with the copper-haired, grey-eyed woman. She's bought that, too. Then she dies.

Guitar has his brief moment when he eschews his "recent asceticism" and fantasizes about what his share of the gold would buy for his grandmother and her brother, Uncle Billy, but then his thinking returns to its cold-blooded groove: "Guitar smiled at the sun, and talked lovingly of televisions, and brass beds, and week-long card games, but his mind was on the wonders of TNT" (SS 181). With the mention of explosives we realize that

Guitar's acquisition fable is not about material goods but about killing. When he soon says, "You know about me—you can guess why I'm in it [i.e. robbing Pilate]" (181), the reasonable guess is that he's doing it to bankroll the Seven Days, or least his part of the mission to keep the ledger of killing balanced. Guitar's fable is about acquiring victims and keeping count; it is about what he calls "Numbers. Balance. Ratio" (158).

But the story goes beyond Guitar being the Sabbath Day of the Seven Days. Milkman does indeed hear "the hunter's horn in Guitar's voice" (SS 184) as they plot to rob Pilate, for Guitar is a hunter, a killer, and was one well before the Seven Days provided an ideology and an outlet for his aggressions. Early in the novel, Guitar tells a story about growing up in the South, and it is a memory about hunting:

> Just listen, Milkman. Listen to me. I used to hunt a lot. From the time I could walk almost and I was good at it. Everybody said I was a natural. I could hear anything, smell anything, and see like a cat. You know what I mean? A natural. And I was never scared—not of the dark or shadows or funny sounds, and I was never afraid to kill. Anything. . . . I'd take a shot at anything. The grown men used to laugh about it. Said I was a natural-born hunter. After we moved up here with my grandmother, that was the only thing about the South I missed. (85)

This is Guitar's favorite memory of the South and his best memory of it. It is the memory that eases the pain of losing his father, it is the memory that guides him to create a self, of his liking, that can deal with the pain of abandonment. It is a self that is, like the little boy he once was, "never afraid to kill."

In one of the most interesting features of Morrison's narrative design, the Virginia chapters at the end are interrupted by a flashback to the morning Guitar borrowed a car and drove

Hagar home, hours after she failed to ice-pick Milkman. In his way, his heart goes out to her, and he says:

> "You know what, Hagar? Everything I ever loved in my life left me. My father died when I was four. That was the first leaving I knew and the hardest. Then my mother. There were four of us and she just couldn't cut it when my father died. She ran away. Just ran away. My aunt took care of us until my grandmother could get there. Then my grandmother took care of us. Then Uncle Billy came. They're both close to death now. So it was hard for me to latch on to a woman, because I thought if I loved anything it would die. But I did latch on. Once. But I guess once is all you can manage." Guitar thought about it and said, "But I never wanted to kill her. *Him*, yeah. But not her.'" (SS 307)

There, that day, in the car, Guitar goes down his whole long list of loss and talks about a woman who was the object of his love. But coming as it does soon after Guitar hunts Milkman and almost strangles him, the passage clearly alludes to Milkman, and to how Milkman has left Guitar, and to how Guitar loves him enough to kill him.

In the last chapter, as Milkman is riding home in a bus from the South, he wonders if he can "defuse" Guitar and at least end the "man-hunt." But "even as he phrased the thought in his mind, Milkman knew it was not so" (SS 330). While he cannot quite figure out the reason—was it the gold? was it Guitar's "work" as a Seven Day?—he knows that Guitar has a need to kill him. Is this about numbers, ratio, balance? Has it been decided that it's going to take the deaths of four white children *and* a black man to avenge the deaths of the four Negro girls in Alabama? These matters cross Milkman's mind. But he is closer to the truth when he asks a different set of questions—is Guitar someone who would save his life, or take it? It is then that he realizes that Guitar could do both. That is acquisitive as well.

At the beginning of chapter 15, the last chapter of *Song of Solomon*, Milkman is so crazy about finding a sweet lady named Sweet, and stumbling upon his own African myth, that he actually becomes a city-bred Negro who can't wait to go swimming in a backwoods, snake-infested Virginia river. Sweet complains about getting in the water, and getting her hair wet, and dealing with the water moccasins. Milkman shrieks:

> "Leave me. Leave me in here by myself. I don't care. I'll play with the water moccasins." . . . "He could fly! You hear me? My great-granddaddy could fly! Goddam!" He whipped the water with his fists, then jumped straight up as though he too could take off, and landed on his back and sank down, his mouth and eyes full of water. Up again. Still pounding, leaping, diving. "The son of a bitch could fly! You hear me, Sweet? That motherfucker could fly! Could fly! He didn't need no airplane. Didn't need no fuckin tee double you ay. He could fly his own self!" (SS 328)

Milkman goes on about Solomon, and Sweet understandably thinks maybe he's drunk. But then she asks questions, which, in the context of the novel's story, are a woman's questions:

> "Where'd he go, Macon?"
> "Back to Africa. Tell Guitar he went back to Africa."
> "Who'd he leave behind?"
> "Everybody! He left everybody down on the ground and he sailed on off like a black eagle. 'O-o-o-o-o-o Solomon done fly, Solomon done gone / Solomon cut across the sky, Solomon gone home!'" (328–329)

With this, we get in detail the African myth of the novel and the African myth that stimulates Milkman to find what sense of self he can find before his young life presumably ends.

So, if African myths are as "contaminated" as the fables of the West, as Toni Morrison suggests in her provocative remarks, what is impure or unsuitable about the African myth Milkman has recounted and joyously embraced? I would point immediately to three concerns, all having to do with the perpetuation of abandonment and survivorhood.

The myth Milkman discovers is a wonderful story insofar as it provides him with genealogy, family pride, and a masculine identity (however outsized). When the children play their ring games and sing the Song of Solomon, the song is no longer a silly children's rhyme, it is his song, and, as he says, "my game." But what if the myth becomes for a Milkman a directive for future behavior? What if he begins to rationalize his treatment of Hagar as "mythic" behavior foreordained by Solomon "lift[ing] his beautiful black ass up in the sky and [flying] home?" (SS 328). What if *that's* his game?

The Solomon myth is a vibrant story in all the ways it creates community choruses. The children in the South who sing and, in a sense, enact the Solomon song in their ring games are one such community chorus. The crowd in the North that gathers to see Mr. Robert Smith spread his blue silk wings and fly is, arguably, another community chorus, especially once Pilate starts singing, *O Sugarman done fly away / Sugarman done gone / Sugarman cut across the sky / Sugarman gone home* (SS 6). And of course, the song has its special place in the repertoire of the community chorus that is the household of Pilate, Reba, and Hagar.

But a myth of departure is a story of people left behind, who do not necessarily become families or communities, let alone communal choruses. Milkman exclaims, "He left everybody down on the ground and he sailed off like a black eagle." "Everybody down on the ground" is just that, no more than that; people left behind. Milkman's new-found family pride and race pride exudes when he claims his great-granddaddy was a "black eagle," but might Morrison also be slyly suggesting that there was something very American about Solomon's black behavior? Certainly, there is something American about the result of what he did.

The Solomon myth is a "good" myth in the ways it rationalizes and explains an unexpected departure. It is a "contaminated" myth if its real and abiding work is to "mythologize desertion."[7] Barack Obama learned to be very careful about telling stories about how his absent African father was a prince (and his grandfather a king), partly because he then had to live with those stories. One wonders how Milkman would have come to live with his Flying African story, or was he living it when he went to Solomon's Leap, and leaped?

Part Two

INTRODUCTION

When Harvard University Press invited me to create an appendix to my Du Bois lectures, I thought at once of gathering together the four essays presented in the following pages. "Sharing the Thunder: The Literary Exchanges of Harriet Beecher Stowe, Henry Bibb, and Frederick Douglass" first appeared in Eric Sundquist's collection *New Essays on Uncle Tom's Cabin* (1986). It discusses how Stowe and Douglass debated their antislavery positions not just in public pronouncements and private correspondence but also in their antislavery fictions, notably Stowe's novel *Uncle Tom's Cabin* (1852) and Douglass's novella "The Heroic Slave" (1853). Henry Bibb and his 1849 slave narrative enter the discussion because of Stowe's queries regarding Bibb in her letters to Douglass, which lead me to observe that there is a strong likeness between Stowe's story of George and Eliza Harris (in *Uncle Tom's Cabin*) and that of Henry and Malinda Bibb. In all, "Sharing the Thunder" offers a portrait of Douglass discovering his beliefs and his voice in the early 1850s through literary exchanges with his peers in the abolitionist struggle. These were, of course, the very years in which he was composing his thoughts for *My Bondage and My Freedom* (1855), the autobiography I discussed in the first Du Bois lecture.

"Willard Savoy's *Alien Land:* Biracial Identity in a Novel of the 1940s" is the foreword I prepared for the 2006 reprint of that novel, first published in 1949. Savoy's story presents in Kern Roberts a biracial protagonist who is male and whose white parent is his mother. Themes consistently discussed in the Du Bois lectures appear in *Alien Land* as well. For example, Kern Roberts struggles to raise himself, with both parents variously absent, after his mother is murdered and his father becomes totally immersed in his legal work (he is what we today would call a civil rights lawyer and activist). Kern also spends much of the novel seeking a home elsewhere, first his deceased mother's private rooms and finally in the secluded spaces of Vermont, where he is close to his maternal grandmother and near his mother's grave. To be sure, Kern does attempt an adoption of his father's black heritage when as a young man he travels deep into the South to Alabama to live with his father's sister, Paula, and to matriculate at the local black college. But that brave effort is dashed when Paula and her husband, Jake, are murdered. When Kern flees Alabama, he flees his black heritage as well; but that is not as resolute as it appears, since Kern's father is also biracial. Race is complicated for Kern.

What I gain from rereading *Alien Land* [in the Age of Obama] is a fresh understanding of what it means to seek, and to be successful in gaining, an invention of one's racial self that is a self-invention, a self beyond the strictures of the models of living provided by parents and family, especially when the parents and families are of different races. Kern Roberts doesn't quite achieve that self-invention, but he figures out how to survive. Barack Obama survives but achieves self-invention, too, in his narrative and in his life.

"Distrust of the Reader in Afro-American Narratives" was my contribution to Sacvan Bercovitch's collection *Reconstructing American Literary History* (1985). It is the primary essay I wrote in a period in which I was much engaged in assessing and debating the prospects of reader-response criticism for careful readings of African American literature. Put simply, I argue in this essay that reader-response approaches are inadequate in discussions of American and African American literature when they ignore the fact that reading constituencies in America have been formed by race as well as by "economic organization," "social rank," or "institutional or professional position." I go on to argue that African American writers have always been aware of the reading constituencies created by race, and have understandably developed narrative strategies that creatively express an awareness of and distrust of the American reader. This leads me to contend that a distinction should be made between storywriters and writing storytellers. Storywriters, by and large, accept all the modernist notions about the irrelevance of the reader, and write accordingly. Writing storytellers are attracted to the idea that readers are, when engaged by good writing, story listeners, or something very close to that ideal.

I include this essay in the appendix because I think of Toni Morrison as being a "writing storyteller," and because I think this is a feature of her craft that Barack Obama admires and emulates. With each writer, the first thing to see is the compulsion to create, through energized, imaginative writing, a readership that is collaborative and supportive of the storytelling. Narratives that create collaborative readers, readers who are, in a profound sense, story listeners, are, if you will, community-organizing narratives.

"A Greyhound Kind of Mood" appeared in *New England Review* (Winter 2001) and was a Notable Essay of the Year for 2001. It is a memoir of 1962–1963, my first year of college, and as such, it is an account of "schoolhouse lessons" in race and class, complete with something to observe of the roles of adults in these episodes. World events impose on this schoolhouse story when I attempt to describe how impossible it was to study and sit for a final exam in philosophy on the very day of the August 1963 March on Washington and Martin Luther King, Jr.'s "I Have A Dream" speech. (Why I was in summer school in the first place is yet another part of this sorry tale.) "A Greyhound Kind of Mood" is obviously in conversation with the second Du Bois lecture, which discusses schoolhouse episodes in texts by Du Bois, James Weldon Johnson, and Zora Neale Hurston, as well as in Obama's *Dreams from My Father.* It has a special place in the appendix in that, as a memoir, it affords me an opportunity to commune with the classics in all of the "voices" in which I work.

A GREYHOUND KIND OF MOOD

Despite all the chest-thumping, pep talks, and pronounced strutting the summer before, I didn't get through my first year of college too well. I don't think I quite got over the first day when a campus gardener in the shadows threw rocks at me, rocks that landed closer and closer, as I walked to the library. At the time, I said to myself, "Good, my man, you didn't even flinch." But I did some flinching later, when I found out that all sorts of other bombardments were in store.

There were some triumphs, including the mysterious ones in which the fellows who were evil to me mostly flunked out, perhaps because I had called their names while rubbing my mezuzah and chanting the Apostles' Creed, usually in the shower. But mostly, the assaults predominated, and some were self-inflicted. I did a bang-up job on myself in English, for example. My English professor was a nut-case who could drift into soft laments about how much Hawaiian Punch his profligate children were consuming, but he was scary, too. He menaced by manner, and by reputation (this was the guy who had flunked out Edward Albee), and he had had a tart greeting for me ("I don't like anybody from the University of Chicago, even from its high school").

When this guy assigned the first essay, I got to work on it way early, on a Saturday afternoon no less, punching out ideas and turns of phrase while my roommates were bumping and shrieking and getting toasted down at the football game. I got pay-

back: a good grade and a grudgingly respectful comment in
return. But did I play it smart and work just as hard on the rest
of the essays? No, of course I didn't. I was too dumb to be that
smart. In those days, I could even convince myself that an essay
begun six hours before the deadline—at the *end* of an all-nighter—
just might be the "best ever."

But some matters were, it seemed, completely beyond my
control, even if I studied, and in the hands of larger forces like
the fates and furies who arbitrarily save or doom a swimmer, a
motorist, a gambler. With a sixteen-year-old's logic, I had enrolled in an engineering drawing course, thinking it might prove
useful if I ever became an architect, which made as much sense
as thinking that I'd better take a religion course just in case I
became a priest. (I did the religion course the next year.) To be
sure, I'd thought I was prepared for such a course since I had
studied mechanical drawing (we called it "macdraw") in high
school. But nothing in "macdraw" readied me for drawing with
precision the guts of turbines, hydraulic pumps, and the like. I
had excelled at a kind of cartography: Ask me to map a farmer's
fields? Let me at it, I can do it—in four colors, even. But what
are these pumps, these cylinders and chambers, these bolts,
these gray masses of steel? Nothing in my work experience or
school training gave me a clue.

Another problem was the "coterie problem," to put the matter genteelly: drawing classes of this order are peculiar institutions for male bonding. Certainly this was so in my high school:
us guys ("macdraw" was only guys) were allowed to banter and
even croon a tune, as long as we kept drawing, finishing the
problem sets on time. While I was never one of the good-time
boys who went off on Wednesday nights (a school night, imagine) to Chicago Blackhawk games, I was still a part of the inner
circle, a circle that did not exclude too many people, because if
you had had the nerve in our school to sign up for "macdraw"

instead of a second foreign language or an extra term of history, well, you were "in."

I know I sought a comparable circle in my college's engineering drawing course; I know I thought that finding such a circle would ease my way into college life, a thousand miles away from home for the first time. There was a circle there, all right, but it excluded me. In this, all my classmates and even my instructor were in cahoots: they weren't hostile to me, but they ignored me, since their greater, consuming project in bonding was to build something that allowed them to stand up to the preppies and the patricians at the college who (whether in fact or fantasy) questioned their presence. Engineering drawing was, in short, a haven for white scholarship boys from the working classes, complete with an instructor with hard-won, G.I.-bill, undistinguished degrees (but no Ph.D.), who identified with all "his boys," except one. Once they started in on the adventures of customizing '57 Chevies and how many transmissions and tires they went through in a year, I knew that my walking into this course was just like Ellison's Invisible Man's stumbling into the white union meeting at the Liberty Paint Factory: he wanted to be friendly and get his lunch from his locker, I wanted to be friendly and earn my grade. Neither of us had any idea how complicated our simple missions would turn out to be.

To be fair, the instructor did visit my drawing table every now and then, like once a month, and to be honest, I was peculiarly (and fatally) satisfied with the Bs and Cs I was getting on drawing the machine innards I had never known existed. These weren't the grades I'd received in "macdraw," but hey, I wasn't getting the kind of grades I'd received in high school in most of my courses. In most of my courses, as the term rushed to a close, there were still opportunities for success and redemption: the paper you could write over Christmas break, the January exam that could slightly lower your grade but also maybe raise it, too. In engineering drawing, we were presented with the ultimate crapshoot: there would be an exam, there would be three problems to draw, there would be no partial credit. In other words, there would be an exam, and there would be four grades possible: 100, 67, 33, and 0.

After Christmas break, we arrived back to find final exam schedules almost gleaming in our mailboxes. One look at the schedule told me that my crazy assortment of courses had run one more number on me: because of what I was taking, I was to have five exams in three days. Too young to be crafty, too numb to think straight and ask a dean to spread the exams out, too imbued with a near-archaic philosophy of Uplift that commanded, "Be stoic and meet this challenge; this will make you a better man to meet the Man," I went ahead and planned a kamikaze study schedule in which for some exams I could review for a day, and for other exams, perforce, several hours.

In the process of deciding which exams most needed my best hours, best thoughts, I found myself perplexed, sidetracked even, at a time I most needed to be focused, by the anomaly represented by the engineering drawing exam. Why the crapshoot? Why tell a bunch of young boys, already anxious about making it through college, that one cold January morning, the dice were going to roll relentlessly for three hours, and that at the end of that morning, some Cs would be As, but more likely, some As would be Cs, and some Cs would be Fs?

I went again to the instructor for some final, clarifying advice about how to prepare. He said: "There is no way to study for this exam; either you are prepared or you aren't." Then he grinned and, while running his hand through his severe crewcut, like an NCO fingering the groove of his power in the military, he added, "And remember, no partial credit!" I sighed and departed, knowing that even if he had straight-up told me exactly what to study, I needed to spend most of my few, waning hours reviewing calculus. That course was in jeopardy; but that exam I could study for.

The booby prize for sitting for five exams in three days was that you were suddenly free, free for three whole weeks before the next term began to, say, ski the Alps or at least Vermont, or to lie on some white-sand beach, marveling at how the green of the sea met the blue of the sky, while mild winds wafted a jaunty red-hulled boat home to a friendly port. In my case, I packed a bag for returning to arctic Chicago, and made my way to the Greyhound station, knowing that it was much too soon to ask my folks for airline tickets or even train tickets, since they had just shelled out that kind of money to bring me home for Christmas. But also, even without knowing how I'd done on my exams, I was in a Greyhound kind of mood: I was going home with my tail between my legs.

The thirty-hour ride through two snowstorms, the crazed driver with the glittering rodeo belt buckle who fishtailed us through slick New Jersey and Pennsylvania turnpikes, muttering how his bus "wasn't ever gonna be late," the near-predictable grope from the sawtoothed man who danced through the bus to sit beside me in New York to chat me up, the ridiculous furlough with miserable food in South Bend, maddening to endure when we were less than two hours from Chicago; these episodes were worse than I expected, but all that I deserved.

When I returned east to college weeks later, I found my grades, in the private confines of my mailbox, but also publicly posted, which was something I had never encountered before, and never imagined would occur. While some professors, mostly the younger ones, courteously posted final grades with only a student's initials beside each grade (that seemed courteous at the time), others just let everything hang out, old school: Avery—B; Brown—C+, and so forth.

Midwesterner that I was, this seemed a procedure imported

from jolly old England, something from the same crate that produced the kindly old parson doing his best to chaplain a modern-day American college. It reminded me of old films I'd seen, perhaps Mr. Chips films, in which a gaggle of English public school boys yipped around a posting of exam results, all of them jumping up and down, straining to see who got what and, more particularly, who was about to be sent home. Home, in that carriage which in the films arrived always on the most miserable rain-sodden day, with a driver, rain-chilled to the bone, who is so sorry, as he soon conveys, to be transporting young Harry (or young George, Edward—you know, the kingly names) home to inevitable disgrace. All this came to me while I jostled with classmates before the boards with our results, myself thinking, "But young Harry can go off and become an officer in India; what am I to do?"

My grades ranged from B+ to F: the B+ in history, the F in engineering drawing. While I had done well enough to escape academic probation or any other serious reprimand, I had an F on my record that had to be made up; I was a course short. When I called my mother with the news, from the sequestered telephone booth in the library I preferred for calls home, she was quick to quip, "Now, I know that school gives out a *variety* of grades, but you didn't have to go and try to get one of *each!*" Her blues humor made me chuckle, and in chuckling I knew we both were hurting.

A morning or two later, I sat up in my dorm bed with a jolt; a ray of light had pierced through the cloud cap of my insistent numbness: I hadn't yet retrieved all of my final exams, and of all of those, I suddenly knew I had to see, read, feel, and read again the exam for engineering drawing, the exam which apparently caused my grade to plummet from some kind of B (at worst, C+) all the way down to F. Anger pushed me around the room as I found clothes, shoes, and threw on a jacket. Then I descended down the hill to the engineering building.

Since it was early in the morning and still between terms, I thought I might just enter the building, locate the pile of exams, find mine, and retreat. But it wasn't that easy. As I grabbed my exam and turned to depart, I came face to face with my instructor, standing about nine feet away.

"You failed my exam," he said, point blank. I stood in silence, trying to gauge his tone, hoping I had heard concern, fearing that I had heard glee.

"Yes, I guess I did, seeing how you flunked me," I countered. He didn't like that, and he twitched a bit, running through an assortment of gestures and smiles.

"I guess you don't care," he offered, with one of the smiles. That got to me. "Don't care?" I raged to myself; "Don't care???"

I thought about hitting him, I honestly did. I didn't think about what he could probably do to me, with one hand tied behind his back, or about how striking out would just play into his plans; I just wanted to smash him, hard. But then I remembered something, and it was neither a piece of scripture nor an elder's pungent warning but a scene at a high school basketball game. I was on the bench, so I had a front-and-center view of a moment when a guy on our team named Larry lost it and broke the nose of a ref who'd been riding him, calling the smallest fouls. Blood gushed and blanketed the ref's white-and-black shirt; the ref screamed; the crowd howled, too. It took a police escort for Larry—and the rest of us—to get out of that gym and onto our bus. Larry was the only guy on our team destined for serious college basketball, but one punch wiped that out. Larry was not just expelled from school but whisked out of the state. I looked at my instructor, whose gesticulations of disbelief at my failure were surely designed to taunt me, and I said to myself, "I'm not going to be no Larry."

Composed finally, I folded my exam once, twice—more than I needed to in order to fit it in my jacket pocket, but as much as I needed to, otherwise. Then I walked with purpose, for the door out of there was straight ahead. I readied myself for another catcall, another baiting, from the now flushed instructor, as I marched toward the door out. I expected further taunts, no doubt, because on my first college day the thrown rocks had come closer and closer, as I approached the door in. But further taunts never came. Apparently, for my instructor, my rush to the door, to what he hoped the rest of the campus held in store for me, was satisfaction enough.

What awaited me at my dorm, in any case, was a bellowing sophomore, swollen with rage, marauding the hallways, breaking the few things breakable in the miserable cinderblock corridors. He had gotten his grades, too, and he had flunked out, and he was pissed and planning, planning his last night at the college.

A few of us stopped and watched him (but not as we would observe him later), for he was the living embodiment of something we all feared. To look at him was to stare at flunk-out, which was something worst than failure; to observe his behavior was to wonder how does one behave on one's last day at college, should that day occur? Maybe he was passing on to us the stages of some ritual, some hallowed college tradition not entirely unlike the other mumbo-jumbo we freshmen had been obliged to witness since September. I considered: was this part of the code of going out like a man? There were other things to do that day, but I, we, were keeping an eye on Alfred, the sophomore.

Around eight o'clock that night, right when my frosh cronies and I were about to make our weekly Saturday trek for hamburgers and the encounters with the girls we fantasized were waiting for us at the local Friendly's, Alfred arrived in the halls with a young lady. Giggling, they disappeared into his room, tipsy, with Alfred roaring warnings to her about stepping over a half-packed suitcase. A woman in the dorm was illegal, we knew, but it was, as we knew, too, Alfred's Last Night. So we winked and smirked, and strutted off to Friendly's.

Screams were lasering the corridors when we later stepped back onto our dorm floor, and they weren't screams of passion. But then, as dumb late-adolescent boys, as freshmen in more than one sense of the term, we weren't sure, so we crept closer to Alfred's door, and listened some more. But what, really, were we listening for? And if the young woman was really being raped, what were we prepared to do?

Three of us, all midwesterners at an eastern college (a detail that still seems important), stood in the hall near Alfred's door, staring at each other, wringing our hands, reeling with the screams, animated yet paralyzed. Then Alfred opened the door and strolled out, strangely more sober than before but now drunk with success. He strolled buck naked with a shit-eating grin, holding aloft a bloody condom. We were young men, too, quaking with testosterone, but we shrank away. Alfred cried, "Hey, guys, c'mon, looka this!" But we wanted no part of it.

The two juniors on the hall arrived, no doubt from fraternity doings. I had often wondered how they had ended up in our dorm, which was mostly a freshmen ghetto. They were both from Boston and had been tight friends since prep school. One was Jewish and the other a Waspy blueblood, and frankly I was amazed, then, that they were so comfortable with each other. Ben was the guy who finally asked me why I wore a mezuzah; Charley was the one who called me "boy" once too often, and had laughed and laughed when I called him out for it. It was offered as locker-room banter, but I had deep suspicions. Puzzled, he had replied, "Don't you know how much I like you?"

Unlike the rest of us, the juniors did not shrink away from Alfred. They cornered him and cuffed him, and Ben threw him in the shower. Alfred flailed and spat, spewing Ben with all sorts of motherfuckers. He also called Ben a stupid kike, which he'd probably been dying to do all semester. Ben just pushed-punched Alfred back into the icy stream of water. It was as if he were doing a slow-rhythm exercise with a punching bag. The blond guy from California, the one who'd had a Volvo engine on his desk all the past semester, and auto parts instead of pencils in the desk drawers, disgustedly quit trying to shave and left the bath area to Ben and Alfred and their battling.

Charley saw to the woman, once she appeared in the hall, clothed, her coat fiercely wrapped and belted. Charley had a car and offered her a ride home. He later told us that she was a high school senior, and that she had asked him to drop her off at the school dance where she was supposed to have been all along. He told us that the next day, late in the afternoon, after Alfred had packed and had slunk to the railroad station. And after someone had finally done something about the bloody condom on the shower room floor.

Years later, when I was a senior, I was walking home from my fraternity after a sorry Saturday evening of drinking beer and singing along to the jukebox. In the shadows, I ran into a woman I knew only because she was a regular at parties at the fraternity next door. That was also the only way she knew me. She was crying, not in a moping way, but in a kind of magnificiently pissed-off way. She had a strength.

But something was wrong, perhaps terribly wrong. I held back from asking because I thought that asking might lead to helping, and that didn't seem wise. I thought about how Charley had helped that girl on our corridor freshman year, and I knew that something similarly gallant was probably called for now. But I held back. She knew me as the "colored guy" the guys liked, but I knew "the guys," and still had deep reason to distrust what they might think of me playing Charley, helping one of their damsels in distress.

But when she said, "Can you help me get home?" I nodded, and indicated the direction of my parked car. We drove out of town on Fairfield Avenue, then got onto the Berlin Turnpike heading south. As we passed the McDonald's, I muttered to myself, "Not too far out of town, please, not too far out of town." I wanted to think she was too upset to speak, but in truth she was too pissed off to speak. When a sniffle or a sigh welled up, she snuffed it. Tough lady, I thought. When she spoke, she gave directions. I grunted "okay" and slowed down and exited the Turnpike as she told me to do.

We were deep in Berlin—a town with a name that didn't bring me the happiest of associations—when she said, "Turn here." "Here" was a short dirt road, leading up to a house with a tiny porch light I could see beyond the ship-size tractor trailer parked along the way. Spying the truck, she said, "Shit, my father's home." I swore, too, but for my own reasons. Fifty yards later up the dirt road, she pressed my right arm and whispered, "Stop here, turn around!" Swiftly, I did so, cutting off my headlights as well.

"Thanks." That word came my way in a humidity of breath. Then in one fluid motion she both kissed me and fled out of the car into a trudge up the dark dirt road. I stayed the instant long enough to catch a glimpse of her in my rearview mirror, then accelerated and roared out of there, switching on the headlights between quick shifts of gears. As it turned out, town and another beer before bed were only twenty minutes away.

Spring came and with it the few last hurdles to finishing freshman year and getting the hell back to Chicago. I was doing better in my courses, mainly because I was steering clear of engineering drawing and everything else having to do with engineering (I never set foot in that building again until it was turned into a bookstore decades later). I filled that course slot with another history course, the B+ in history first term having seduced me into thinking that I was bound to be a historian. My expectation was that the last hurdles would be the obvious ones, the final papers and exams, but I was wrong, and so too were a couple of other greenhorn frosh on my corridor.

One guy had convinced himself that his professors were too distracted—either by their scholarship or by their dementia—to trundle off to the dean's office and record class absences in the Cut Book, a conspicuously displayed ledger of such size and weight that I figured that it, too, had come over from nineteenth-century England in that crate that brought the chaplain. Of course, that guy turned out to be colossally wrong: his professors were entering him in the Cut Book as regularly as they ate breakfast. He was in trouble.

Another guy suddenly got fed up with the absurdity of what was officially the only proper way to turn in a paper: a paper was to be folded in half, never offered flat, with the fold lengthwise, not crosswise, with your name at the top of the folded paper. This was a silly thing to get upset about, but then, it was a silly thing to require. Plus, even a freshman could tell that the professors who were real sticklers about this were the few remaining idiots left over from when colleges were run like boarding schools. Cajole them and move on!

But this guy said to himself, "I gotta know: is my paper going to read for what it is or for how it is folded?" He obsessed about this, turned in a good paper folded wrong, and got his answer: "C+, but this would have been blah-blah if you had done blah-blah-blah." We on the corridor talked into the night about that.

Ted from Pittsburgh was a particular friend of mine. We talked a lot, and when Easter Sunday came along, we pooled together the extra cash our parents had sent for the holiday and had a mighty fine Easter dinner in a good restaurant on Maple Avenue. So, I had a special worry when Ted decided that he could not in good conscience sign the pledge, to be entered in yet another huge ledger, that he had indeed attended at least eight chapel services in the first semester.

All of us on the hall tried to reason with him. Some guys said *meaning* to attend chapel eight times was enough. Others said walking *by* the chapel eight times was enough. One guy proposed that if Ted had gone to chapel a couple of times, walked by the chapel a couple of times, talked to the chaplain a couple of times, and maybe gone to a wedding or a funeral some time or another in the last year, then surely Ted could sign the pledge. That sounded good, super good; we whooped it up. But Ted wouldn't budge. He tested the code. And he found himself in trouble.

As for myself, I was the guy who got incensed about the writing proficiency exam. This exam was the spring rite that made certain that no freshman entered the sophomore year without being able to write an essay. Never mind the fact that we had by that point in the year written a dozen essays. There would be a day in May, no doubt a perfect May day, with pleasing blossoms and airy hints of summer's heft, when the freshmen would file past the razzing upperclassmen and disappear into a dim and dusty hall to write *proficiently.*

Even the older guys who liked to see freshmen suffer gave us the dope on this exam: keep it simple. Simple ideas, simple sentences; forget about attempting nice phrasings or using punctuation other than the period; forget about trying to *write.* As one guy put it, "Your model for this essay is not Henry James; it's Dick and Jane."

I heard all this and swore I'd "Dick and Jane" my way through. But I got into the exam, read the topic I was to write on, and I found myself thinking about something I had just read in the *New Republic*. One voice in my head was yelling "Do Dick and Jane!" and it was sounding a little anxious, because another voice was whispering, "Hey guy, write a gutsy reply to the *New Republic;* don't demean yourself by writing some simple shit." I got fired up, and wrote my rejoinder to the *New Republic* piece with blinding, fatal speed.

I really thought I had written a fine essay, and was seriously thinking of typing it up and mailing it to the magazine as soon as I got it back. So convinced of my accomplishment was I that I was shocked when my name appeared on the list of those students who had to take the exam again, and stricken when I was informed that I was to appear before the board of English professors who had graded the exam.

Once before the board, I was asked how I came up with the idea for the essay. I launched right in by telling them that their topic reminded me of an article I had just read, and that the article had contended x and then y and z. One professor cut me off right there and asked what that article had to do with the essay I had written. Startled, I said, "Why, my essay was a response to the article, and a way of taking on your topic—which I did, didn't I?" The professors glanced at one another; one took what looked like my essay from the top of a pile and started thumbing through it.

Desperate, I started up again. "Look, that article was about something your topic brought up. I addressed your topic by taking up that specific case. . . ." I got no further because the professor chairing the meeting held up his hand. "We thank you for your explanation," he began. "We called you in because your essay was unusual, and we were puzzled." I was puzzled, too, and didn't know what was coming next. "We thought perhaps," and he paused, then said, "you had tried to memorize some-thing and offer it as your essay." Young as I was, it took me a day to realize that he was telling me that I had been called be-fore them because they thought I might have plagiarized.

With the plagiarism question "cleared up," I was still told that I had to take the exam again. In writing, I had made, in their estimation, more than the allowable number of punctua-tion errors. Terrorized by this inquisition, I sat for my second and last chance to pass the writing proficiency exam, and with a certain numbness I wrote "Dick and Jane" prose as if I were in grade school again. And I passed. But I still wonder: how did I forgive and forget enough to become an English major two years later?

Going home to Chicago I took the train, bus travel being too long and lonely, air flights being too short and bourgeois, or so I thought then. I traveled with some of the Midwest boys going home to places like Waterloo, Iowa and Decatur, Illinois, and also with a soulful guy named Mark, who'd be sitting in coach all the way to his home in Seattle. I didn't envy him that. Sitting up on the train for just one long night, with only the chatter of friends and the fireworks of the occasional steel mill hulking out the window to amuse me, was one night too many for me.

When the train arrived at the southside Chicago Englewood station, I debarked, leaping off and then back onto the train to retrieve my bags, my books, my tennis racquet, my pool cue. Debarking at Englewood made simple sense in that it was the station closest to home. But the choice was a little more compli-cated than that. For while I was acting out some kind of bra-vado (of which the pool cue was a prop), playfully enacting for my schoolmates still on the train the role of "Southside Bobby," an unlikely fiction I'd made of myself for them back East, I was also making almost fatally sure that I was getting off the train at a place where I couldn't catch a cab. Deep down I knew that since white folks had now pretty much stopped getting off the train at Englewood, almost no cabs lined up there anymore. But I refused that. I said, a cab will be there for me. I said, my Chicago won't do me that way. But it did me that way, and I started making phone calls, searching for someone to pick me up.

I forget why my folks couldn't come get me and why Charlie Runner picked me up. But that was all right, and fitting, since all I knew and loved about trains and their sounds and velocity-size-power I had learned at dawn at Englewood Station when Charlie would take me there as a small boy to see the Twentieth-Century Limited and the Broadway Limited (the crack New York Central and Pennsylvania Railroad trains) fly down the rails, straining for more speed, racing each other for the finish line in Chicago's Loop.

The trains would tornado by, throwing off hellish heat and stinging gravel, causing me to half-hide in the folds of Charlie's Korean War trenchcoat. But Charlie would turn me out of his coat to make sure I saw things, like the Pullman porters leaning precariously out of each careening competing train, flapping towels at each other, woofing at each other.

I thought about those porters when I spotted Charlie's car approaching and I waved and waved until he saw me and he waved back. We were managing another rendezvous at Englewood Station, before it and the trains he'd taught me to *see* were totally things of the past.

Days later, I started working at Provident Hospital, where my father was born, where I was born, and where I had worked before. I was put to work in the pharmacy, counting pills, mixing mouthwash, picking up and delivering prescriptions on the hour on each floor. But during my lunch hour, I found myself hovering in the emergency room, craving the unexpected like the painted baby they brought in one day.

The baby had been born "right black," as the old folks used to say, but was painted a hellish yellow when it arrived, screaming, the thick paint still glistening yet hardening, burning and clogging the infant's pores. The white ambulance guys were too amazed by this yellow-wet baby to fall into their usual, casual, here's another messed-up Negro sign-here mode. They moved swiftly, not caring if their uniforms got smeared with the yellow goo. Most of the emergency room attendants swooped toward the howling baby; a few others noticed the baby's mother stumbling out of the back of the ambulance and drifting toward the hospital door. They gathered her in and seated her before rushing to join the rest of the crew, who were trying to figure out how in hell to remove the layers of oil-based paint, however sloshed on, that were eating into the skin of the baby.

Attention fell to the baby: you can't pour paint remover on a child; besides, we don't have paint remover. Will simple alcohol do? We can dab and dab and wipe and wipe, but can we relieve this child? Can we do it quick enough? I was just six feet away from the situation, and I heard professionals for the first time in my life sounding anxious and uncertain.

Because I was as immersed as the emergency people were in trying to save the baby, I was as jolted as they when a shout rang out from the emergency sitting room. Nurses were racing toward the painted baby's mother. Even as they swooped to surround her, forming a flapping human tent about her, I could see that she was undressing herself. I saw her deep brown breasts come into plain view, I heard the pulsing moan that spewed from her lips while her eyes rolled and got wild.

With birdlike motions, one nurse flicked and tucked a gown about the mother, pushing the gown further into place. Another nurse bent close to the woman, touched her swaying forehead, asking, "What's the matter, dearie, what's wrong?" The swaying mother kept tugging at the straps and buttons beneath the gown, mumbling all the while, "I gotta go home and paint myself, I gotta go paint myself." Then her moans set in again. The nurse made a quick motion. Catlike, someone slipped through the circle, toting a huge syringe. The wild-eyed mother of the painted baby was promptly drugged, and within seconds it seemed, she slumped, stone out cold.

That mother. I still think of her and still invent stories for her that lead up to her and her baby ending up at the Provident emergency room. In one story, she has decided to paint her baby and has spent the morning looking for a can of white paint. She wants white paint because, for all the old, sorryass reasons, she thinks the baby will be better off white. But as the blues say, she got trouble, trouble, every day, every way, and all she can find, all the Good Lord can *put* her way, is some yellow paint. And she totes that paint up into her apartment and over to her baby's crib; and she slathers the yellow paint on real good, just like she would glaze a ham. The baby was already crying; it's really screaming now, and the more it screams the more the mother dips and paints, humming while she works. A neighbor bursts in, "What's going on here? Why's that baby screaming?" she says. At the sight of the baby, she herself screams. Bustling down the hall, she goes and calls the ambulance. The mother puts down the brush and inspects her child. Not white, she thinks, but not black either. And maybe she thinks too that the screams are of a different color now.

As the sole pharmacy assistant that summer, I had my hands full, and my days full, too. At first, there was the romance of "entering the real world" and joining the rank and file down at the bus stop for the thirty-block jostle to work. Then, too, I liked my pharmacy white coat, just like the ones the real pharmacists wore: you could really strut and pretend in that. But soon I got tired of getting up at dawn, and tired of being tired at the end of the day. Sometimes I'd be so tired that I'd get home and take a nap so deep that my mother couldn't wake me for dinner. When that happened, she'd leave a plate of food for me to eat later. But sometimes, I'd sleep through the evening and the night and not get to that plate until breakfast time.

Clearly, I was not just exhausted, I was depressed. But "depression" was not a term I used then or fully understood or thought could possibly apply to me. (I was too young for depression but old enough for college, right?) It was a term I allowed myself to recognize in aptitude tests or to deploy in American history essays, but otherwise it could not be a part of my vocabulary. To admit it in the door, so to speak, would be to admit all sorts of things, like the demons who appeared in my dreams, howling and hooting. I'd scream at them, "What are you laughing at?" A voice would reply, "Where do you want me to start?" and howl some more.

In the midst of this engulfing stupor, my mother one day reminded me not only that dinner was ready but that I was to start summer school that evening. Summer school! Of course, I hadn't really forgotten it, for how could I forget why I had to go? I had flunked engineering drawing and had to make up the credit. But here it was, and so soon. I wanted to go back to sleep, but I ate something and borrowed my mother's car to dash to class.

Only as I drove north on Stony Island and then into the gentle curves of Jackson Park did I begin to assemble a reasonable recollection of what course I had signed up for and why. It was a philosophy course to be taught by a University of Chicago professor I'd vaguely heard of named Walker Sawyer. The topic was pre-Socratic philosophy, which was already a puzzle since it was news to me that philosophy had existed before Socrates. But I figured everything would be okay since "Walker Sawyer" sounded impressively intellectual and I had noticed his books in the bookstore. And besides, the class was going to be in the same downtown building where I'd gone to prep for the SATs. This was going to work.

When you are young you think you can learn anything. It is just a matter of cracking open the book and reading long and hard. When that works, you believe you have "applied yourself." When it doesn't work, you consider you might be stupid. Of course, since even the most self-punishing of us has strategies for avoiding the cloaca of stupidity, there are recourses such as blaming the instructor (as in "Walker Sawyer is a know-nothing prick") or blaming higher education ("I hate school!"). But when I fell asleep at home while trying to read philosophy for the first time in my life, or fell asleep in Professor Sawyer's class, or went to sleep in my mother's car instead of going to class, even when parked just a block away from the classroom building, I didn't fault Walker Sawyer. And it never occurred to me to "hate school." I just wanted to sleep, and sleep.

At the end of August, I quit my hospital job several days early, thinking it was time to "wake up" and study for my philosophy exam, especially since the whole grade would be determined by that final exam. I pored through my books, filled out my 3 x 5 cards, and gobbled the snacks my mother would bring up to my room. It was like old times, like the best days of high school. My class notes were, to say the least, cursory, and there was no class chum to call for help because I hadn't learned anybody's name, let alone made any friends. But I was working and it was coming together, according to plan.

On the third day, the day of the exam, my plan called for a final six-hour push, which would end around four p.m., giving me plenty of time to shower and eat and relax before the exam at seven. I set to studying early enough that morning, but there was an odd feeling about the house. For one thing, the television downstairs droned on, well after the end of the morning news shows. After I'd worked a couple of hours, I went downstairs for a fresh cup of coffee. The television was still on, and my mother was transfixed before it, still in her robe, which was unheard-of.

"What's up?" I said. "King's march on Washington. It's really happening," she replied, barely turning toward me.

I peered into the television screen. I walked a few steps forward to get a better view. Look at all those people on the Mall; there must be thousands and thousands. "Look, there's Harry Belafonte," I exclaimed, inching closer. But then I jumped back. No, no, no, Bobby, I said to myself. You have an exam tonight. You have mucho studying still to do. This may be Martin Luther King's march but it's the Devil's work: the Devil wants you to fail and this is his great temptation. In just this way I talked myself back to my desk.

I studied some more, then came downstairs again, looking for lunch. I was prowling in the refrigerator when my mother sighed, "I never thought I'd see this day." She told me the estimates of the crowd, and as if to corroborate her, the television flashed another panoramic view of the seas of people flanking the reflecting pool. She rattled off the names of the politicians and celebrities. We marveled at which white folks had shown up, mentally entering their names in an honor roll. She told me who had already spoken and who had been good. I tried to make a sandwich while listening to my mother *and* Walter Cronkite, while riveted by images of people, a rainbow of people, some stylish in suits, some militant in overalls, all swept up in the cause, all sweeping me far away from who philosophized what before Socrates had his say.

"I'll call you when King speaks." Promising that was my mother's way of sending me back to my books. And I went. But now I was wondering how Professor Sawyer could possibly have scheduled his exam the same day as the march. How unfair!

How unaware! Was he so ensconced in his ivory tower that he didn't see the conflict? Didn't he want his students to watch the march—maybe even *go* to the march? Why hadn't he rescheduled, why hadn't we students petitioned that he reschedule?

We students. I shouldn't have gone there in my flailing about. I didn't need to be fuming about *what kind of people* could study ancient philosophy *during* the March on Washington, and who could take an exam as if nothing else were going on in the world that day. And it was not helpful at all for me to begin considering that I wasn't a real student, the proof of it being that I could let King and all the rest distract me, hopelessly. But I considered that, and considered, too, that I had studied enough. Knowing that wasn't right, I studied thirty minutes more. Then I closed my books and, taking my fate into my own hands, went off to listen to Martin.

My philosophy grade arrived a few weeks later to my college mailbox in the East, the same mailbox that had harbored so many other momentous messages in less than a year. I had passed! I had said to hell with studying, and I had joined the huge flock in Washington—no! the million-fold brethren around the world!—who had gathered to hear Martin preach. With them, I followed Martin to the mountaintop; with them, I shouted "Amen!" to Martin's "I Have a Dream, for *all* God's children!" Yes, I had heard all that, I was *there* for that. And by golly I had passed philosophy, too.

But it turned out that passing wasn't enough. As a dean explained, the college only accepted grades above C from other institutions. Stunned, I just stared at him while it sank in on me that I was still a credit short, that somehow I had to try all over again to make up a course. For an instant, I thought about telling the dean that the philosophy course only required a final exam and that the exam was on the very day of the March on Washington and that, and that. . . . But even I knew what that would sound like, especially coming from one of the college's five black students. So I gathered myself and went my way.

I thought about going to the library to call my mother with the news. But I didn't. I didn't need to start the new year by contorting myself into the telephone booth, which before had been my favorite place for reporting disasters. And I didn't need her blues laugh, for I had learned my own. The voice in my head wasn't churning through some blues now, though; it was chanting. And the words were, "Martin, Martin."

5

SHARING THE THUNDER

The Literary Exchanges of Harriet Beecher Stowe,
Henry Bibb, and Frederick Douglass

In an October 1852 number of *Frederick Douglass's Paper* appears a book notice entitled "Stolen Thunder." Briefly described therein is W. L. G. Smith's *Life at the South; Or Uncle Tom's Cabin as It Is,* one of the many books that followed close on Harriet Beecher Stowe's novel in an attempt to gain a corner of the market *Uncle Tom's Cabin* had singlehandedly created. In regard to Smith's book, "stolen thunder" has a double meaning, for, according to the reviewer, Smith is not just attempting to "make money out of the popularity of 'Uncle Tom's Cabin'" but also seeking "withal a little capital for the 'patriarchal institution.'"[1]

"Stolen thunder" aptly describes most of these publishing ventures, particularly those that were shamelessly entrepreneurial and those pursued by white Americans, even when, like Stowe, they vilified slavery. But the phrase falls short of the complex relationship between Stowe's novel and the many Afro-American antislavery texts published in the late 1840s and early 1850s. Some of these appear to have followed the stolen thunder pattern: Solomon Northup's *Twelve Years a Slave* (1853), for example, was dedicated, with great flourish, to Stowe ("whose name, throughout the world, is identified with the GREAT REFORM") and was generally promoted—and received—as "another key to Uncle Tom's Cabin" or, as one newspaper put it, "Uncle Tom's Cabin—No. 2."[2] On the other hand, the relationship between *Uncle Tom's Cabin* and *Twelve Years a Slave* is not a simple one of promotion and sales or of two products vying for the same finite market. The two narratives share internal features that bind them together in literary history: When Northup divulges the existence of a thriving slave market in the nation's capital city, exposes the brutal forms of slave life in the Red River region of Louisiana, or rehearses the figure of Stowe's George Shelby in his own "saviors" from the North (Henry B. Northup of New York, but also the Canadian, Samuel Bass), he is not so much stealing Stowe's thunder as substantiating the antislavery literary conventions established (if not exactly invented) by her—all the while telling his own story, of course. *Uncle Tom's Cabin* did not provide Northup with his tale or his stance against the "peculiar institution," but it may well have affected his autobiographical acts of remembering. In this regard especially, the relationship between Stowe's and Northup's works is both complex and literary; the textual conversation between the two narratives prompts the idea that Stowe and Northup shared the antislavery thunder of the 1850s: despite the activities of his white editor and amanuensis, David Wilson, Northup cannot be said to have poached on Stowe's success.

The relationship between *Uncle Tom's Cabin* and Frederick Douglass's novella "The Heroic Slave" (1853) provides an even more interesting study of antislavery textual conversation, partly because Douglass, unlike Northup, was easily Stowe's equal as a prominent antislavery activist and partly because Douglass and Stowe knew each other and corresponded repeatedly during the period in which their antislavery fictions were being composed. Although dedicated alike to the task of eradicating slavery and to other causes such as the promotion of temperance, Stowe and Douglass differed profoundly on certain related issues—for instance, African colonization and the extent to which the American church community had succored slaveholders and hence abetted slaveholding. Although they debated these matters directly in their correspondence, and indirectly in public pronouncements, it can also be said that they conversed further in the pages of their antislavery fictions. The features of this exchange—of this sharing of the antislavery thunder—are explored in the rest of this essay.

In July 1851, a scant month after the Washington, D.C., *National Era* had begun its serialization of *Uncle Tom's Cabin,* Harriet Beecher Stowe wrote Frederick Douglass a rather spirited letter. She began politely with a request for Douglass's assistance in acquiring accurate information about the details of life and work on a southern cotton plantation, but soon thereafter shifted her subject and tone, taking Douglass to task for what she understood to be his critical view of the church and of African colonization. Both parts of this letter tell us something about the composition of *Uncle Tom's Cabin* and are suggestive as well about what may be termed the countercomposition of "The Heroic Slave."

Stowe's request of Douglass is expressed in this way:

> You may perhaps have noticed in your editorial readings a series of articles that I am furnishing for the Era under the title of "Uncle Tom's Cabin or Life among the lowly"—In the course of my story, the scene will fall upon a cotton plantation—I am very desirous to gain information from one who has been an actual labourer on one—&—. it occurs to me that in the circle of your acquaintance there might be one who would be able to communicate to me some such information as I desire—I have before me an able paper written by a southern planter in which the details &. modus operandi are given from *his* point of sight—I am anxious to have some more from another standpoint—I wish to be able to make a picture that shall be graphic &. true to nature in its details—Such a person as *Henry Bibb*, if in this country

might give me just the kind of information I desire you may possible know of some other person—I will subjoin to this letter a
list of questions which in that case, you will do me a favor by
enclosing to the individual—with a request that he will at earliest
convenience answer them—[3]

Above and beyond what I sense to be a remarkable admixture of
civility and imperiousness, two features of this statement war-
rant mention. One is that, although Stowe was undeniably an
armchair sociologist of the South, here she appears to be rather
assiduous in gathering southern testimony and in seeking the
forms of black testimony that could both counter and corroborate the white testimony she already had in hand. The idea of
weighing white and black testimony alike in order to gain a
"picture" of plantation life that is "true to nature" was probably
anathema to most white southerners of the late 1850s. But
Stowe's practice here shows clearly that, contrary to the opinion
of many southern whites (including Mary Boykin Chesnut), she
did assay southern views, white and black, while composing *Uncle
Tom's Cabin.*

The other signal feature is Stowe's reference to Henry Bibb.
Bibb was a Kentucky slave, born probably in 1815, who escaped
from bondage only to return repeatedly to Kentucky to rescue
his family as well. None of his efforts met with success; indeed,
at one point, Bibb was recaptured and sold "down river" with
his family to slaveholders in the Red River region. Further attempts to escape as a family were also thwarted. Eventually, Bibb
once again escaped on his own, arriving in Detroit, but only after additional trials of bondage, including a time in which he
was the property of an Indian slaveholder, and after another
brave effort to save Malinda, his wife, which ended when he
discovered she had become her master's favorite concubine.
Bibb's account of his story was published in 1849 under the title

*Narrative of the Life and Adventures of Henry Bibb, an Ameri-
can Slave, Written by Himself;* it was undoubtedly one of the
principal slave narratives discussed in antislavery circles during
the period in which *Uncle Tom's Cabin* was being composed
and first serialized.

Interest in Bibb's narrative continues today. Gilbert Osofsky
included it among the narratives collected in *Puttin' On Ole
Massa* (an anthology that, along with Arna Bontemps's *Great
Slave Narratives,* introduced a generation of fledgling Afro-
Americanists to slave narratives other than Douglass's of 1845),
and I have elsewhere discussed its particular narrative strategies.[4]
Among its enduring features is Bibb's story of his Indian captivity, an account that places the narrative in the popular tradition
of captivity narratives and that, however obliquely, touches upon
a key issue of Bibb's day—whether the practice of slaveholding
should be allowed to expand into the Indian Territories, especially once they had become states of the Union. Another key
feature is Bibb's love for and dedication to his still enslaved family, particularly as repeatedly expressed in his willingness to venture back across the Ohio River, deep into the bowels of danger,
in order to attempt their rescue and release. His portrait of
family unity against the odds (unity up to a point—since, as we
know, Bibb was eventually compelled to abandon them) unquestionably struck a chord with the abolitionists of the 1850s,
who brought it forth as further proof of slavery's sinful assault
on the slave's effort to maintain a semblance of Christian home
life. Moreover, it is one of the accounts that has encouraged
historians of our time, including Herbert Gutman and John
Blassingame, to insist that the slave family could and did, in
Gutman's words, "develop and sustain meaningful domestic
and kin arrangements."[5]

A third feature, as central to Bibb's narrative as the portrait
of family life, is his caustic view of the complicity between the

church and the institution of slaveholding. Although Bibb is presented by his guarantors—abolitionists in Detroit—possibly out of necessity as a member of a Sabbath school and a man of "Christian course," it is clear in the body of *his* text that he has been variously wounded by the conduct of American Christians, and that as a result he is suspicious of them and "their" church. Fairly early in the *Narrative*, for example, Bibb makes his way back south in quest of his family, but is captured by a mob of slaveholders and soon imprisoned in Louisville. Of the mob, he says:

> In searching my pockets, they found my certificate from the Methodist E. Church . . . testifying to my worthiness as a member of that church. And what made the matter look more disgraceful to me, many of this mob were members of the M. E. Church, and they were the persons who took away my church ticket, and then robbed me also of fourteen dollars in cash, a silver watch for which I paid ten dollars, a pocket knife for which I paid seventy-five cents, and a Bible for which I paid sixty-two and one half cents. All this they tyranically robbed me of, and yet my owner, Wrn. Gatewood, was a regular member of the same church to which I belonged.[6]

Much later in the narrative, after Bibb and his family have been sold into an abominable state of bondage in Louisiana, he records the following about his new master, a church deacon:

> And while I was offering up my prayers to that God who never forsakes those in the hour of danger who trust in him, I thought of Deacon Whitfield; I thought of his profession, and doubted his piety. I thought of his handcuffs, of his whips, of his chains, of his stocks, of his thumb-screws, of his slave driver and overseer, and of his religion; I also thought of his opposition to prayer meetings, and of his five hundred lashes promised me for

attending a prayer meeting. I thought of God, I thought of the devil, I thought of hell; and I thought of heaven, and wondered whether I should ever see the Deacon there. And I calculated that if heaven was made up of such Deacons, or such persons, it could not be filled with love to all mankind . . . as we know it is from the truth of the Bible.[7]

In light of these pronouncements, grounded as they were in the most bitter of experiences, it is not surprising that Bibb claims elsewhere in his story that "I never had religion enough to keep me from running away from slavery in my life."[8]

Finally, Bibb's *Narrative* endures as much for its figurative language as for its rhetoric and ideology. I refer here to Bibb's descriptions of the Ohio River (which separated freedom in Ohio from bondage in Kentucky) as a road to freedom and, for the bonded black, a river Jordan. The most remarkable passage in this vein begins:

> Sometimes standing on the Ohio River bluff, looking over on a free State, and as far north as my eyes could see, I have eagerly gazed upon the blue sky of the free North, which at times constrained me to cry out from the depths of my soul, Oh! Canada, sweet land of rest—Oh! when shall I get there?[9]

As the passage concludes, Bibb's language reminds us first of Frederick Douglass's earlier description of the images of freedom offered by Maryland's Chesapeake Bay, and then of more contemporary imaginings, such as those moments in John Edgar Wideman's *Brothers and Keepers* (1984) when he explores the irony of his brother's incarceration in a prison (called "Western") along the banks of the Ohio:

> I have stood upon the lofty banks of the river Ohio, gazing upon the splendid steamboats, wafted with all their magnificence up

and down the river, and I thought of the fishes of the water, the fowls of the air, the wild beasts of the forest, all appeared to be free, to go just where they pleased, and I was an unhappy slave![10]

I have quoted at some length from Bibb's narrative principally to suggest that Mrs. Stowe's interest in it may not have been limited to Bibb's account of life on Red River cotton plantations (for which, see his chapters 10–12). At the very least, I would argue that her portrayal of Eliza Harris's escape to freedom across the ice patches of the Ohio River was prompted in part by Bibb's high symbolism of the Ohio as a pathway of freedom. It also seems clear that Bibb's allegiance to his family gave impetus to Stowe's portraits of the Harris family and of Tom's family as well. It also seems altogether possible that Stowe's George Harris is a fictive Bibb—in his light skin, which would have abetted his escape, and in his vociferous allegiance to family, his vivid dreams of freedom in Canada, and his occasional grave doubts about the social and moral efficacy of Christian practice.

In short, Stowe's story of George and Eliza Harris is roughly that of Henry and Malinda Bibb, once a happy outcome to the Bibbs's plight has been, as some nineteenth-century pundits liked to say, "bestowed." Altogether, Stowe's debt to Bibb's *Narrative* is as great as that she incurred while reading another 1849 narrative, *The Life of Josiah Henson, Formerly a Slave, Now an Inhabitant of Canada, as Narrated by Himself.* Much has been made over the decades, some by Stowe herself, of Tom's resemblance to Henson, and of how Henson's escape to Canada may have inspired Stowe's presentation of the Harrises' settlement there. But when we study the texts alone, it is clear that the parallels between George Harris and Bibb are as pronounced and that Bibb's experiences on a Red River cotton plantation probably had as much to do with the composition of *Uncle Tom's Cabin* as did Henson's escape to Canada. Indeed, Harris in Canada is something of a Henson and a Bibb, much as Tom in Louisiana is both a Bibb and a Henson.

If Stowe's novel favors Henson's text, the evidence is in her treatment of the two subjects that take up the balance of her 1851 letter to Douglass. Having made her request of him and referring to Bibb in the process, Stowe writes:

> —I have noticed with regret, your sentiments on two subjects,— the church—&. African Colonization—&. with the more regret, because I think you have a considerable share of reason for your feelings on both these subjects—but I would willingly if I could modify your views on both points.[11]

Nothing comes of her intention to debate Douglass's criticisms of African colonization. But in what remains of the letter, she is thoroughly impassioned in defending the church: she is, as she says, a minister's daughter, a minister's wife, the sister of six ministers, and she thereby chooses to take questions of the church's stand on slavery as in some measure charges against her own and her family's conduct. Having defended herself and her kin ("it has been the influence that we found *in the church & by the altar that has made us do all this*"), Stowe ends her letter in this way:

> After all my brother, the strength &. hope of your oppressed race does lie in the *church*—In hearts united to Him. . . . Every thing is against you—but *Jesus Christ* is for you—&. He has not forgotten his church misguided &. erring though it be. . . . This movement must &. will become a purely religious one. . . . christians north &. south will give up all connection with [slavery] &. later up their testimony against it—&. thus the work will be done—[12]

Given these views, it is not surprising that in *Uncle Tom's Cabin* Stowe created both Tom and George Harris, and chose to present them, albeit in rough, nearly unrealized fashion, as a kind of bifurcated, black antislavery hero—one almost white, the other very black; one hot-tempered, the other stoic to the point of meekness; one impelled by circumstances farther and farther north, the other farther and farther south; one central to her narrative ideologically, as an emblem of African colonization, the other central spiritually, and hence the "better half" of Stowe's hero, since he is emblematic of exalted Christian faith. The curiosity of this construction is that, although Tom is the "better" and true hero of Stowe's novel, whose character and presence create strong ties between her own and Henson's text—ties that would endure well into the remainder of the century through the other publishing activities of Stowe and Henson alike—it is in George Harris, not Tom, that Stowe confronts what were for her and other white Americans the most troubling issues in the antislavery debate, and confronts as well the tone and argument of the more problematic (though doubtless inspiring) slave narratives of the late 1840s: those of Bibb, Douglass, and a few other miscegenated hotheads. In Tom, Stowe expresses her consuming respect for Henson. In George Harris, she creates a composite portrait of Bibb, Douglass, and the rest of their type; and although she honors them throughout the bulk of her long novel, judiciously imagining how they, had they been Harris, would have responded to a given crisis or turn of events, she also sends them packing, first to Canada and then to Liberia. In short, the paragraphs on African colonization missing from Stowe's letter to Douglass are to be found in the chapters of *Uncle Tom's Cabin* that she would write soon after. She revises the close of Bibb's *Narrative,* where it is evident that he resides not in Canada but (still) in the United States, and replies as well to Douglass's many criticisms of the church and colonization alike, suggesting that he might just consider, in light of his views, removing not merely from Boston to Rochester, as he had just done, but from the Afro-American's New World to his Old.

Much as Stowe completed her letter in the pages of *Uncle Tom's Cabin,* so Douglass responded in his written account of the slave revolt hero Madison Washington, whose story he had offered many times in the 1840s, here and abroad, in oral tellings. Known as "The Heroic Slave," the novella shares certain features with Stowe's novel but also challenges her text, especially in its presentation of a black hero as dark-skinned as her Tom (apparently magnificently so) and yet as rebelliously violent and skeptical of the American church as her George Harris. In this regard, and in its hero's "self-extrication" from the United States to the Bahamas, Douglass's novella of 1853 converses with Stowe's novel and replies to her 1851 letter, written during the composition of *Uncle Tom's Cabin.*

"The Heroic Slave" was written as Douglass's contribution to *Autographs for Freedom, a* publication created by the Rochester (New York) Ladies' Anti-Slavery Society to subsidize *Frederick Douglass's Paper* (known prior to 1853 as the *North Star*). Stowe herself was a contributor: she submitted an "autograph" and also took part in certain editorial activities, as the following 1852 announcement of the society suggests:

> . . . we intend to publish an anti-slavery annual. . . . It was first designed to name the book, *"The Anti-Slavery Autograph;"* but the gifted authoress of *"Uncle Tom's Cabin"* has christened it *"Autographs for Freedom;"* and we willingly accept her baptism for the forthcoming volume.[13]

Douglass shared the society's regard for Stowe and her novel. In a March 1853 account of a visit to the Reverend and Mrs. Stowe at their Andover, Massachusetts, home, Douglass remarks on what he perceives to be her modest demeanor and then writes:

It is only when in conversation with the authoress of *"Uncle Tom's Cabin"* that she would be suspected of possessing that deep insight into human character, that melting pathos, keen and quiet wit, powers of argumentation, exalted sense of justice, and enlightened and comprehensive philosophy, so eminently exemplified in the *master book* of the nineteenth century.[14]

Soon thereafter, Douglass developed a set piece of praise for *Uncle Tom's Cabin* and its commanding international influence, which he worked into many speeches, no matter what the occasion or topic. In one version of the piece, Douglass implores that a fugitive slave act be passed every day of the week, so that "fresh feelings and new editions of *Uncle Tom*" may be created.[15] In most other versions (of 1853 and 1854), he argues that the American abolitionist movement cannot be thwarted, either by silencing its speakers or by burning its books, including Stowe's novel:

They might cut out my tongue, and the tongue of every abolitionist in the States north of Mason &. Dixon's line; they might disband every anti-slavery organization in the land; they might gather together all the tracts, pamphlets, and periodicals ever published against slavery; they might take "Uncle Tom's Cabin" out of the ten thousand dwellings of this country, and bring them all into their splendid capitol—in their magnificent metropolis, Washington—and there set fire to them, and send their flame against the sky, and scatter their ashes to the four winds of heaven; but still the slaveholder would have no peace.[16]

Douglass's praise of Stowe was, I think, variously motivated. For one thing, he truly respected her gift and accomplishment, perhaps especially so in 1852 and 1853, when he was wrestling with the written version of Madison Washington's story, a story he had told orally, but usually quite sketchily, many times. (The doubts of a beginning fiction writer are surely expressed when Douglass says of Stowe in 1853, "We are all looking for examples, and we look for them among the great ones; if we cannot imitate them in their great works we can, at least, imitate them in their manners and bearing.")[17] On the other hand, we should acknowledge that Douglass praised Stowe partly because he wanted something from her—her support, including that of a monetary nature, for one of his pet projects of the 1850s, an industrial college for black youth, preferably to be located in his newly adopted city of Rochester. Douglass never realized the project, as we know, though the dream was fulfilled decades later when Samuel C. Armstrong created Hampton Institute and Booker T. Washington later founded Tuskegee. But while the school was still a possibility, Douglass praised Stowe publicly and for the most part chose to debate their differences "in conference" or, if publicly, often circuitously. His most ingenious act of circuity was, as I have been suggesting, "The Heroic Slave."

In comparing *Uncle Tom's Cabin* and "The Heroic Slave," one sees immediately which antislavery literary conventions the works share. Unlike most novels of the 1850s, but clearly in anticipation of the work to come from Mark Twain and the local colorists, both works offer an almost formidable display of American vernaculars and dialects, issuing from white and black characters alike. Stowe and Douglass differ in their pursuit of this convention in the range of vernaculars attributed to blacks. In *Uncle Tom's Cabin,* the gamut runs from the standard English of George Harris (hardly the vernacular of a racial character) to the folksy, if not exactly broken, speech of, say, Aunt Chloe: "Missis let Sally try to make some cake, t'other day, jes to *larn* her, she said. 'O, go way, Missis,' said I; 'it really hurts my feelin's, now, to see good vittles spilt dat ar way! Cake ris all to one side—no shape at all; no more than my shoe; go way!'"[18]

In Stowe, the various black vernaculars reinforce what she suggests in other ways about black stratification according to color, ambition, employment, geographical location, possibly gender, and, quite often, given name: The most degraded slaves in the novel, such as Simon Legree's black accomplices, Sambo and Quimbo, are in name, speech, and sensibility "African residuals," whereas Tom, Emmeline, and others are, by contrast, to be received as Afro-Europeans of some order, their names functioning as indicators of the plausibility of their high feelings, unswerving religiosity, and fierce moral convictions.

Douglass proceeds in another fashion, preferring the voice of a single slave hero to an exhibit of the sociolinguistic range of a race. On the other hand, his strategy is similar to Stowe's in that his black hero's name—Madison Washington—is as much a sign of his literacy as it is of his state of origin (Virginia), his credentials as a revolutionary, and his quintessential Americanness. One result is that Madison's speeches, not unlike some of George Harris's, are overwrought and hence not "true to nature," except perhaps in being much like some of Douglass's addresses and those of Virginia's other famous sons. Another result, much in keeping with Douglass's predilections and activist strategies, is that every serious discussion of slavery in the novella is conducted on a dignified level, each speech exhibiting grammatical correctness as well as social courtesy, especially when the exchanges are between blacks and whites. We turn to other, presumably lower, levels of American conversation only when whites discuss slavery among themselves. Here Douglass employs diacritical simulations of American speech, not to suggest the condition of the lowest blacks but to characterize the lowest whites—those who are, in effect, confreres of Stowe's Simon Legree and who speak his language, or worse.

Stowe and Douglass also shared an interest in American symbolic geography as seen from the slave's point of view. This leads, in both fictions, to a meticulous presentation of the geography of freedom, which focuses on Ohio as well as Canada. As suggested before, Stowe picks up where Bibb leaves off in depicting the significance and risk of a slave's managing to cross the Ohio River—recall here Eliza Harris's leaping from river ice patch to ice patch while grasping her child, in flight from her would-be captors. But whereas Bibb is altogether scant in portraying his north-of-the-Ohio benefactors, including Mr. D_____, perhaps because he fears compromising their service to other escaping slaves, Stowe works up an elaborate study of Senator and Mrs. Bird, who assist Eliza Harris, and of the many Quakers who eventually help the Harris family as a whole.

Unlike Stowe and Bibb, Douglass does not pause in "The Heroic Slave" to sketch the northern banks of the Ohio as freedom's green shore; eloquence of that sort and for that subject is reserved instead for the prospect of safety on British soil, in Canada and later the Bahamas. However, the state of Ohio is, for Douglass, unquestionably a portion of freedom's realm, less because of its famous southern river than because of the brave souls residing there who choose to aid fugitive slaves. In this regard, he proceeds quite differently than he does in his 1845 *Narrative,* where he is very circumspect about how he escaped and about who, if anyone, assisted him: he joins Stowe in offering what are probably thinly veiled protraits of active abolitionists and their families. Douglass's Ohio abolitionists, the Listwells, turn out to be an *economical* creation as well: they constitute a composite portrait of helpfulness, understanding, and antislavery zeal, not only because they probably represent many actual abolitionists but also because they perform all the tasks and express all the feelings that Stowe distributes among at least three groups—the Birds, the Shelbys, and the Quakers.

In their presentation of social spaces, Stowe and Douglass proceed rather uniformly. For both, the striking contrast between model domestic settings and the seamy affairs of tavern life, repeatedly and variously elaborated, is a principal means of clarifying phenomenologically the distinctions between good and evil, heaven and hell, family life and other coarser, possibly "unnatural," arrangements, and the right and wrong sides of the slavery issue. In "The Heroic Slave," Douglass's strategy is as simple as it is effective. At the heart of the novella, much is made of the contrast between the Listwells' Ohio home, where Madison Washington finds comfort and aid, and the appointments inside and out of a Virginia tavern frequented by loafers and slave drivers. Quite to the point, the tavern had once been a house, complete with outbuildings and other physical features suggesting the honorable pursuit of animal husbandry and agriculture. But now the property bears the "ineffaceable marks" of "time and dissipation": "The gloomy mantle of ruin is, already, outspread to envelop it, and its remains . . . remind one of a human skull, after the flesh has mingled with the earth."[19] The fact that the tavern was a home before it became a setting for knavery and intemperance allows Douglass to build his comparison in relentless detail. Barn is compared with barn, hearth with hearth, good housekeeping with its absence, nourishing food with debilitating drink. Even the dogs are made use of, Listwell's faithful Old Monte being an obviously better companion than the listless hounds that lie about the tavern. Douglass varies his strategy in the final section of the novella, where two Virginia sailors discuss the *Creole* revolt and the slavery question in general in a tavernlike setting. Although the scene rehearses to a degree the conversation between Listwell and the loafer in the earlier Virginia tavern—and is indebted particularly to the singular exchange between George Harris and his former employer, Mr. Wilson, in what is perhaps Stowe's most important tavern episode (chap. 11)—it takes on its own ideological character in Douglass's insistence that the place is not a tavern but a coffeehouse. Possibly because of his temperance movement activities, Douglass refused to join Stowe in suggesting, even in fiction, that serious discussion could take place in the presence of alcohol.[20]

Stowe's tavern episodes—recall that she begins the novel with one—are as numerous as those of model domestic life, and the two settings pair up accordingly. We are thus led to compare the elder Mr. Shelby, in a "dining parlor" with the brandy-drinking Haley, with Shelby at home in the company of his virtuous wife. Likewise, the tavern scene depicting Haley and his henchmen is answered in the activities and serious, moral talk of the Bird household, and the tavern discussion of George Harris and Mr. Wilson is followed by the sequestering of the Harrises in the Quaker settlement, a place so domestically harmonious, according to Stowe, that "even the knives and forks had a social clatter as they went on to the table" (chap. 13).

Stowe's most ingenious and ideological handling of these contrasts appears in the Simon Legree chapters—for example, chapter 32, "Dark Places." The description makes clear that Legree's shabby house was once a handsome home, sheltering a family, as opposed to the motley assembly of miscegenated women who variously and sullenly serve him. So, too, we are to understand that its rooms were once used for much loftier domestic purposes than the drinking bouts Legree now conducts in them. In short, a once proud home is now something of a brothel and much of a tavern; in this regard, it is fair to say that Legree's degraded domicile is the model for Douglass's Virginia tavern. Stowe's great touch involves not her descriptions of dissipation but her resolution of these affairs by the captive women. Weakness for drink delivers Legree into Cassy's hands and softens him for the stratagems she works against him. Although Cassy's success does not fully restore domesticity to the Legree household, it does allow her and Emmeline to have a "home of their own" in the upper rooms that Legree dares not enter.

Despite such sharings, Stowe and Douglass created quite different fictions, the differences reflecting contrasting views on the church and colonization as well as the portrayal of black heroism. On the latter score, one may observe that the primary features of Bibb's *Narrative* that Stowe chose not to rehearse are, in fact, reproduced in Douglass's novella. For example, the heroic return from safety to danger in quest of captive kin is undertaken in *Uncle Tom's Cabin* only by white near kin, like young George Shelby, seeking Tom's release. In contrast, Douglass's hero, like Bibb's persona, undertakes this task himself, traveling south from Canada to a slave state, undergoing recapture and reenslavement, and suffering as well the loss of a wife when he regains his personal freedom. Tom is not reunited with Aunt Chloe any more than Bibb and Washington are reunited with their wives, but at least in their versions of the common tale of slave families torn apart, it is the black male family co-head, and not a white surrogate, who seeks reunification.

Moreover, whereas Stowe acknowledges black skepticism about the church's role in the fight against slavery but relegates all such concern to her secondary black hero, George Harris, Douglass, like Bibb, locates this skepticism in the character of his primary hero. That skepticism even touches Listwell, Douglass's primary white hero, who remarks of Washington:

> to him those distant church bells have no grateful music. He shuns the church, the altar, and the great congregation of Christian worshippers, and wanders away to the gloomy forest, to utter in the vacant air complaints and griefs, which the religion of his times and his country can neither console nor relieve.[21]

Listwell obviously is an abolitionist of a different stripe than the Beechers and the Stowes. He is, in brief, a western abolitionist, not a New England one; at the very least, he completes Douglass's vision of such a figure.

Regarding African colonization, Stowe's views appear in the Harrises' successful escape to Canada, their removal thence to France—where George gains the university training he probably cannot receive elsewhere—and their eventual emigration to West Africa to help found a new black society. This is pure Stowe; neither Bibb nor Henson was interested in any such final solution. Nor was Douglass, although in his fiction if not in fact he was keener on forsaking the United States than was Bibb. In "The Heroic Slave," Madison Washington escapes finally to the British Bahamas—that is, to a New World territory free of slavery with a large black population. Washington's presence there, rather than in Africa or Canada, is much in keeping with Douglass's view that, far from submitting to any removal schemes, American blacks should stick together in the New World. As he put it elsewhere, "Individuals emigrate—nations never."[22]

Although Stowe's and Douglass's differing portrayals of black heroism may be seen to arise from their differences about the church and colonization, their handling of the issue of color is also significant here. In *Uncle Tom's Cabin,* Tom is dark and George is fair, a time-hallowed arrangement supporting all the myths of black meekness and white aggression, myths that dictate the heroic qualities of each man. In "The Heroic Slave," Douglass squarely challenges such myths, refusing to bifurcate his hero as well as emphasizing his blackness and valor alike. In this respect, Douglass specifically revises Stowe's characterization of Tom. A comparison of the physical descriptions of Stowe's Tom and Douglass's Washington makes this clear. Here is Stowe's first "daguerreotype" of Tom:

> He was a large, broadchested, powerfully-made man, of a full
> glossy black, and a face whose truly African features were charac-

terized by an expression of grave and steady good sense, united with much kindliness and benevolence. There was something about his whole air self-respecting and dignified, yet united with a confiding and humble simplicity. (chap. 4)

Douglass revises this in his portrait of Washington:

> Madison was of manly form. Tall, symmetrical, round, and strong. In his movements he seemed to combine, with the strength of the lion, a lion's elasticity. His torn sleeves disclosed arms like polished iron. His face was "black but comely." His eye, lit with emotion, kept guard, under a brow as dark and as glossy as the raven's wing. His whole appearance betokened Herculean strength; yet there was nothing savage or forbidding in his aspect. A child might play in his arms, or dance on his shoulder. A giant's strength, but not a giant's heart was in him. His broad mouth and nose spoke only of good nature and kindness. But his voice, that unfailing index of the soul, though full and melodious, had that in it which could terrify as well as charm. He was just the man you would choose when hardships were to be endured, or danger to be encountered—intelligent and brave. He had the head to conceive, and the hand to execute. In a word, he was one to be sought as a friend, but to be dreaded as an enemy.[23]

Tom and Madison are both kind, benevolent, good-natured, and steady, as well as big, handsome, and black. But Madison is also intelligent, brave, possessed of a body promising action and a voice promising speech. Obviously, Madison revises Tom, but the point is that the revision occurs by way of addition to Tom, or rather, to Stowe's portrait of him. Since it can be said that Tom is in his way brave, intelligent, and so forth, the issue is not that he lacks these qualities but that Stowe chooses not to see or remark on them. It may be argued that Stowe in this way creates space for her other, "brighter" hero, George Harris. It may also be argued that Stowe had no such strategy and simply portrayed Tom in the truncated form she wished him to assume. From the latter point of view, she seems, like Garrison and other New Englanders Douglass grew to distrust, the very sort of "blind" abolitionist he sought to enlighten in "The Heroic Slave." Douglass's revision of Tom in Madison Washington not only renders Tom fully visible, it forces abolitionists of a certain, Yankee stripe to see him.

In his essay "Everybody's Protest Novel," James Baldwin argues that Afro-American protest fiction began with *Uncle Tom's Cabin,* and further, that protest fiction has never quite worked its way out of the "cage" Stowe created for it. One feature of that cage is the notion, among black and white protest writers alike, that when God created blacks, He did not do so in His image.[24] Baldwin's argument produces an impassioned assessment of Stowe and Richard Wright, but it does little justice to Douglass's "Heroic Slave." Madison Washington suffers doubts, but not about his blackness: he never sees himself as one of God's lesser children. And it may be that Baldwin did not fully take in the complexity of Stowe either. Tom may conform to Baldwin's views, but Nat Turner does not, and it was Nat Turner and his insurrection that she took up in her next novel. In a sense, Douglass won his debate with Stowe, for he could claim some role in inducing her to write about a black revolutionary. But she won, too: When she wrote about a rebel, she wrote about one—from Virginia—who failed.

6

WILLARD SAVOY'S *ALIEN LAND*

Biracial Identity in a Novel of the 1940s

The publication in early 1949 of *Alien Land,* written by "the newest Negro novelist," as Willard Savoy was dubbed by the *New York Herald Tribune,* met with immediate attention and considerable fanfare. Within weeks, the novel was reviewed in newspapers that included the *Christian Science Monitor, Chicago Sun-Times, Cleveland Plain Dealer, Pittsburgh Courier, Hartford Courant, San Francisco Chronicle, New York Times,* and *Washington Post,* as well as journals such as *Commonweal* and the *Saturday Review of Books.* The reviewers included estimable writers of the day, notably Nelson Algren, Arna Bontemps, and Ann Petry. Often referred to in the commentaries as "Lt. Savoy of the U.S. Air Force" (no doubt in response to the striking photograph of him in uniform on the dust jacket), Savoy was swiftly scheduled for book events ranging from high-publicity book signings at big-name bookstores such as Brentano's in Washington, D.C., to academic events including a seminar on "The Role of the Writer in Building One World" at Fisk University. The "Book Shop" section of the *Crisis* (the journal of the NAACP) offered *Alien Land* from the very moment of its publication; it is striking to see it in the same select fiction list for April 1949 that promotes Dorothy West's novel *The Living Is Easy,* Willard Motley's *Knock on Any Door,* William G. Smith's *Last of the Conquerors,* and Zora Neale Hurston's *Seraph on the Sewanee.*

Alien Land garnered this kind of attention in great part because Dutton, the major New York publishing house, believed
in Savoy and his novel and marshaled the resources to provide a
proper and hopefully profitable debut in public for author and
book alike. The correspondence between Savoy and Dutton
(copies of which have been generously shared with me by Lauret Savoy, Willard Savoy's daughter) reveals a publisher placing
trade advertisements, planning sales conferences, even musing
about seeking blurbs from Sinclair Lewis and Eleanor Roosevelt!
On the eve of *Alien Land*'s publication, Nicholas Wreden, a
vice president of Dutton, wrote Savoy, declaring that "everything connected with the publication of *Alien Land* is progress-
ing beautifully." He went on to remind Savoy that Dutton was
planning to print fifteen thousand copies (three thousand more
than originally intended) and to spend $5,000 on the initial ad-
vertising.

Curiously enough, also on the eve of the novel's publication,
Savoy received a quite different letter from J. R. de la Torre
Bueno ("Bill B") in Dutton's publicity department about a "ba-
sic problem . . . a question." The question was this:

> When interviewers or others say to us, Is Willard Savoy himself
> of Negro extraction?—what shall our answer be? It will have to
> be direct and unequivocal—we will have to say No or Yes. We
> must be ready with our answer ahead of time—the same answer
> agreed to by both parties.

"Bill B" is not entirely happy bringing this matter up; he soon
attempts to address it purely as a business matter ("I don't believe
that either answer will have a marked effect on the sale of ALIEN
LAND"). But then he returns to speaking heart-to-heart:

> the answer could have a profound and lasting effect on your
> whole life and career. Your social life, your Army career, what

else you can guess better than I. In thinking through to your answer, you must bear all possible ramifications in mind; and they are considerably more important to your happiness than to the success or failure of ALIEN LAND. That's why the question is yours to decide about, rather than ours. No doubt you have been thinking of it continuously.

"Bill B" adds that "we'll" need to know the answer in about three weeks.

What does one make of this? Many people at Dutton knew that Savoy was a Negro; Savoy himself was always forthright about this. Even so, was "Bill B" nevertheless considering being coy or evasive about Savoy's race for publicity purposes? Might it be that "Bill B" assumed that the story of *Alien Land*'s "half-white" Kern Roberts is Savoy's story? Does this confusion tell us anything about Savoy's short-lived literary career or about his later reluctance to admit (to his daughter at least) that a literary career or first novel ever existed?

Willard Wilson Savoy was born in September 1916 (Kern Roberts, the novel's hero, is born the same year), in Washington, D.C., a city that is more a charged field than an urban backdrop in *Alien Land* and in a number of pieces he began but never published. His father, Alfred Kiger Savoy, was a school principal and later assistant superintendent of the colored division of the District's public schools. Little is recorded of Savoy's mother, Laura Wilson Savoy; Savoy himself enters her in one document merely as "Laura W., housewife." But there seems to be much more to be said about her in terms of the forging of Savoy's identity and the making of *Alien Land*. For one thing, if Laura Wilson Savoy wasn't white, she was certainly white enough in appearance for her son to imagine, or perhaps more exactly to *experience,* what it was like for young Kern Roberts to grow up with a white mother in black Washington. (Photographs can be deceiving, but to see the photo taken at the Brentano's book party of Laura Savoy *and* her sister Margaret—two white matrons if you ever saw any—hovering above a sheepish-looking Willard is to be convinced that this "black boy" must have had some childhood!)

The omnipresence for Savoy and for his young Kern of both their paternal and maternal surnames also begs attention. Early on in *Alien Land,* a mark of Kern's disavowal of the Negro race is his name change: "He was not Kern Roberts now. Not any more. He was Kern Adams—another, an entirely different person." "Adams" is not a name out of the blue; it is his mother's maiden name; Kern has decided he'd rather be his (white maternal) grandmother's ward than be his (black) father's son. Arguably, Willard Savoy could imagine Kern choosing between "Roberts" and "Adams" because he himself was both a "Wilson" and a "Savoy." He knew well of how living within two names could signify living within a confused—or conflicted—racial identity.

But of central interest here is Savoy's selection of his mother's name, Laura, as Kern's mother's name. Of course, *Alien Land* is fiction, but what are we to make of the fact that the young white woman who marries Kern's (near white) father, births Kern, willingly moves to Washington, "becomes a Negro," and tries to protect her son from the "twisting, tearing forces" awaiting in the District's Negro schools bears the same name as Savoy's mother? Even more remarkable, what unbridled act of imagination might we be encountering when Savoy has young Kern witness the murder of his mother Laura by a brutish black man—in chapter 1 no less? One can only wonder what Laura Savoy thought of all this.

In the world of real events, Willard Savoy did attend Washington's Negro schools, including the famed Dunbar High School, noted for a faculty as well-credentialed as that of many colleges. On the subject of this esteemed faculty, Savoy would later in life [c. 1950s] be quite caustic: "It would seem now that the tiresome rantings of teachers equipped with dusty Masters degrees won on some minor variation of an oft repeated thesis, harked through the years with scant attention to the changes in the world, had a thin virtue." Clearly, young Savoy, not unlike his young Kern Roberts, was contemptuous of the Washington "bona fide Café du Lait society" (which Kern terms the "Association of Oldest Inhabitants") and of the clubs, schools, and churches that supported its aspirations and prejudices. Even so, despite whatever Savoy thought of Dunbar and his fellow black bourgeoisie classmates, he managed a record there that earned him matriculation at Howard University.

He spent most of the 1930s attending college: six years were spent at premier historically black institutions, Howard and Fisk, and he was also a year at the University of Wisconsin. Curiously enough, given the writing and communications careers he later pursued, Savoy was a science student, majoring in organic chemistry. It appears that he did not earn a degree. One is tempted to assume that Savoy was a restless, independent soul in those days, as critical of certain prevailing modes of "striving" campus culture (especially at Howard and Fisk) as he had been of the milieu at Dunbar High. One can even imagine him majoring in chemistry in order to be "responsible" (to himself, to the race) in his studies, as "race men" like Charles Roberts, Kern's father, would insist he be, only to realize that he (like Kern) could not play out that role.

When the United States entered World War II in 1941, Savoy joined the U.S. Army Air Corps. By the end of the war, he was a first lieutenant and lead navigator in the 618th Bombardment Squadron. After the war, he remained in the Air Force until 1949, assigned as a lieutenant to the Press Branch, Air Information Division, with offices in the Pentagon. In the years

immediately before the publication of *Alien Land,* he managed
the Special Interest Unit of the Air Force's Public Relations Division. His work involved preparing copy on the activities of
Negro military personnel worldwide for "use in media types
ranging from TIME Inc., to SEP [Saturday Evening Post],
Reader's Digest, Encyclopedia Brittanica [*sic*] . . . AP, UP, and
total range of Negro print." This is the "day job" that made the
completion of *Alien Land* possible.

The Air Force enabled *Alien Land; Alien Land* was to enable
for Savoy a new life beyond the military. What Savoy sought was
something nearly impossible to find: relief from the daily re-
minders of being Negro in 1940s America. As he poignantly put
the matter in a September 1949 letter to Arna Bontemps: "I do
know that I am looking for several things. . . . One of them is a
respite from the day to day, actively fighting-the-fight which has
been my occupation for the past five years. Another, and certainly related, is the flight to a breathing spell in which personal
dignity may be a thing accorded as a mere matter of course,
rather than given with the grain of condescension one finds
here." Savoy's "flight" would take him to France and to "all of
Asia," where he wrote speeches and news copy for the "Marshall
Plan" Economic Cooperation Administration. By 1953, Savoy
was in Los Angeles, breaking into the "TV game." Television
was to be his "bread and butter" while he finished a new novel
about a Negro artist from a Washington middle-class family.

African American fictions and other narratives often are set in
carefully constructed geographies: freedom and oppression are
mapped; each has a landscape and a climate; each has exterior
and interior spaces to be negotiated. Though there is some suggestion in *Alien Land* that Negroes can be alien, and alienated,
in all of America's geographies, the alien land referenced in the
novel's title is most specifically the American South.

In passages remindful of W. E. B. Du Bois's descriptions in *The Souls of Black Folk* of traveling South ("If you wish to ride with me you must come into the Jim Crow Car"), Savoy first introduces the region by way of portraying Kern Roberts's journey "as a Negro traveler" southward from Cincinnati, then southward still from Nashville, to Valley View, the small Alabama town where he will live with his Aunt Paula and Uncle Jake and attend the local black college. The Jim Crow car is a venue where the Negro is "in his place," where "if his spirit feels the vise of shame drawing in upon it it is helpless." The Jim Crow car, though in motion, denies freedom of movement. How ironic, as Savoy knows full well, that the only trains in *Alien Land* providing Jim Crow cars south of Nashville are the *Dixie Flyer* and the *Comet.* (The names of the trains are like the names of slave ships; "bright" and "ironical," as the poet Robert Hayden claimed in "Middle Passage.") Savoy is also attentive to signage: "Kern's mood changed with . . . the first 'For Colored' sign he had seen." Such signs existed in Washington, but these signs in the deep South were more threatening; they signified that "the land through which he rode was alien and hating." Kern discovers that there are more signs to come, including the big one greeting him at the Valley View train station.

And the land: "Beyond Nashville . . . the rolling, green hills gave way to a broken, rutted land on the face of which long, ragged, narrowing gashes showing red earth, ran upward and out of sight into the hillsides." Once in Alabama, Kern is at first hopeful; the "softness of the night" suggests that Valley View "might not be so bad." But the road out to Paula and Jake's prim and tidy home is a "short grayish strip . . . deeply rutted"; it pitches Jake's little car back and forth. There are railroad tracks to cross and a steep hill to climb. Little wonder that the

air seems to Kern "filled with something strange." Little wonder, too, that something awful is about to happen.

The North in *Alien Land* includes New York City, the principal site of the "Interlude" chapters, which take place in the
1940s and which depict Kern's struggle with his racial identity
as he begins to write (personally as well as professionally) and
attempts to be truthful with Marianne, the white woman he
comes to love. Kern's New York is familiar to readers of modern
African American "passing" novels. His "dangerous" irresistible
trips up to Harlem recall those of Nella Larsen's Claire Kendry
in *Passing* (though not with the same fatal result). Moreover,
like James Weldon Johnson's ex–colored man, Kern, once in
New York, is not merely racially ambiguous but a white man
who has made a little money—who is *also* a black man a white
woman is willing to marry. Uncannily, when both the ex–colored
man and Kern muse at the end of their respective stories about
what it might have been like, in Savoy's words, to be "one with
that tiny band of men—the Whites and Washingtons, Du Bois
and Wilkins and Douglass—men who gave their whole lives to
the fight for a race," we sense that both protagonists can make
the gesture of such sentiment because they are at peace with the
"bargain with Life" each has forged to do otherwise.

Life in New York may have created the ingredients for such
peace, but the site for future happiness is "Home" in Vermont,
with Marianne and daughter Margaret (named in memory of
Kern's mother's mother—note, too, that *Savoy's* mother's
mother *and* sister were named Margaret!). Though not without
its own occasions for disappointment, Vermont is *Alien Land*'s
upper North and moral high ground precisely as Alabama is the
novel's lower South and moral abyss. Vermont is the land of
Kern's mother's people, the Adamses. When Kern flees Alabama
and the violence that destroys the lives of Paula and Jake, he
seeks out Vermont, his grandmother, and close proximity to his

mother's grave. (Kern's grandparents do not get to raise him in Vermont, but they do get to bury their daughter there; Charles, his father, doesn't dare stand in the way of that.) When Kern changes his surname to Adams, it is as if he seeks not only to reclaim New England for himself but also to reenter the Garden, to begin again in an "Adamic" sense. Vermont may be where a distraught Kern rehearses being a white boy snarling "Nigger" after fleeing Alabama at age nineteen (what might therapists tell us about Kern landing on *this* definition of how to become a white boy?), but it is also where he eventually becomes the best person he can be: a "self-realized" man who figures out how to reconcile with his father at the same time that he refuses to be his father's version of a nearwhite black man.

Kern's reconciliation with Charles—after nine years of acrimony and absence—occurs in Washington, D.C. This is in keeping with Savoy accentuating the fact that so much that happens to Kern and to his family occurs in the nation's capital. Not unlike William Wells Brown and other earlier African American narrativists who limn images of slave markets cheek to jowl with the District's halls of legislation and justice, Savoy repeatedly creates courtroom scenes, including a final one in which Charles argues before the Supreme Court, that dramatize how elusive justice is for the Negro even in a venue like the capital, where one would hope it would be most accessible. At the other end of the spectrum from the high court, at least in terms of solemnity, is a District Negro barber shop—the Tuxedo Tonsorial Parlor—which Savoy (with considerable ethnographic prowess) also fills with speech. A mark of Savoy's talent and his politics is that the "dozens" boomed by the barbershop patrons are as witty and soulful as the court orations by the Negro lawyers are sonorous and eloquent. In either venue, the ur-text is the narrative of being, as one barbershop brother puts it, "Jim Crowed in the Capitol [*sic*]."

Above all, one must note what befalls the Roberts family personally as a result of Charles having chosen the nation's capital as the site of his family's new "Negro" life. Washington, D.C., is a charged field in *Alien Land* in great part because it is a stage. Charles outwardly rails against acting and the theatre when son Kern shows an adolescent's passion for it, little realizing that he himself is playing a highly scripted role as a light-skinned civil rights lawyer who has suddenly discovered his blackness. Moreover, Charles is hardly prepared to accept that in coercing his white Vermonter spouse to play the role of a Washington Negro wife and mother, he may well have imposed the circumstances that led to her violent death.

In chapter 1, Laura Roberts is fatally in the wrong place at the wrong time because she has been desperate to see her one childhood friend residing in Washington, Dorcas Kuydendahl, in order to share with someone she knows and trusts her despair over Charles's determination to send Kern to the Negro schools (in essence, she fears that her son will become as much as stranger to her as her race-absorbed husband has become). On their way home, while traversing that part of the park (Rock Creek Park, no doubt) that leads to the streetcar that makes "the rattling journey down the long winding hill along 'You' Street, teeming with Negroes," Laura and Kern are separated, and Laura is accosted, groped, and stabbed. Dorcas, who has walked part of the way with them, hears Laura's cries, and is soon on the scene. Taking charge, Dorcas orders that Laura be transported to the Netherlands Embassy, where Dorcas lives and her husband is secretary.

This in itself is an extraordinary "geographical" expression of the situation. Best friend Dorcas determines that Laura, in what remains of her life, doesn't need to be in a white hospital, with her husband screaming at her for "passing," or in a Negro hospital, futilely playing the Negro mother right to the end. Dorcas's

arrangements for her dear friend are a gift: an opportunity to let
Laura live her last hours in what is in effect another country, a
small space in small remove from the race wars decimating the
nation, the nation's capital, and Laura's family.

Laura Roberts's death occurs specifically in 1927. Why that
date, we might ask? One reason is so that we might understand
that the preceding seven years of racial turmoil afflicting Washington and the Roberts family in particular are those that
erupted right at the end of World War I, especially once the
black troops returned. Willard Savoy would have been especially
mindful of such tensions having just recently served in—and returned from—World War II. Another reason for the date is so
that we can know quite specifically that Kern is age ten or eleven
when he witnesses the assault of his mother, is cuffed by the assailant, and is brutalized at school for identifying a black man as
the assailant (however true). He is also of this age when he begins the sorry remaining years of his childhood being raised by
an absent father and Nettie, a spiteful colored housekeeper who
seems to have transferred her contempt for Kern's mother to
Kern. (A key moment in the story thread concerning Kern's
fascination with the theatre involves Nettie saving and mischievously presenting to Charles a playbill that "convicts" Kern of
"passing" at a "white" theater in order to see a production of
Hamlet. Shortly thereafter, Kern assaults Nettie's boyfriend,
surely wanting to beat *her*—for her every intrusion, including
sitting in his mother's chair.)

Savoy may also have chosen 1927 because no year more epit-
omizes the successes of the Harlem Renaissance. And so, if you
are Savoy, an aspiring African American writer in the 1940s, determined like Richard Wright and Chester Himes, among others, to declare a new project well removed from what you deem
the tepid aesthetic of the Renaissance 1920s, you might well
begin *Alien Land* with a killing in Washington instead of a gay

Harlem party. (A related matter is that *Alien Land,* like many of its contemporary texts, is a swing-era novel virtually bereft of music: it seems beholden to the concept that even a whisper of music will entertain, not edify, and hence dilute the message.) The 1940s-style aesthetic project to which Savoy aspires is well expressed when the barber at the Tuxedo Tonsorial Parlor supports Kern's desire to become a writer by declaring, "We need writers. Need people to tell our story to the world. To tell the truth—tell when we right and when we wrong. . . . Every people need that. Too few of us do it. Dunbar and Johnson and those—good enough for their time. But things are changing now and we need to tell today's story. Got a few men like Hughes and Cullen and such telling it in poems. But that ain't good enough. We still need the cold facts told in writing."

This opinion clearly privileges prose over poetry and "cold facts" over whatever might be construed in writing as warm and less than factual—feelings like sentiment or compassion. If this is indeed Savoy's own opinion, too, it confirms that he was in his own way of a number with Richard Wright and Frantz Fanon, writers he studied and admired. And it explains why Savoy, like Wright and Fanon, would write of the anger and madness besetting the Negro in what are often clinical terms. There is more than one instance in *Alien Land* when a black man's rage at his circumstance, often expressed in the most poignant personal vernacular ("You take 'n take 'til you feel murder build up 'n you gotta go—or die"), reads like something coldly impersonal—like clinical transcription. This is because Savoy, like Wright and others, believes that there is fundamentally nothing in the Negro's individual experience that does not bespeak a larger, national American malaise. Even what seems unique in the life of Kern Roberts is, Savoy would argue, a story to be anticipated, given the race rituals of the national culture.

While *Alien Land* shares features with the African American fictions (and nonfictions) of its time, it does possess its own singular attributes, which invariably challenge one or another protocol. For one thing, the novel is in its own way at times frankly sexual or erotic. In one of the Interlude chapters, for example, the evening gets late and Kern ends up spending the night at Marianne's apartment. The episode, including the "morning after," is tastefully offered; when Marianne whispers "You are home," she expresses the love in both their hearts. But still, the fact is that two unmarried people have just bedded each other; one is white and the other, Kern, is a quadroon Negro. The episode is challenging in its time, notably in insisting that interracial sex may be simply and disarmingly human, and not inevitably violent or criminal.

More extraordinary, however, are those moments in *Alien Land* when Savoy's gorgeous women of color parade through, like a bevy of 1940s pinups in a lonely soldier's calendar. Kern expects his Aunt Paula to be "a dour old maid"; imagine his astonishment when he discovers her to be "a willowy, tall girl, with a wealth of shining black hair . . . a golden brown girl . . . an unusually beautiful young woman." The element of repetition in this passage in itself expresses Kern's wonder. And there are more intoxicating young ladies to come, including the demure Adoriah (note the name!) whose eyelashes, olive skin, flowing hair, "Indianlike" cheekbones, and beguiling smile are mesmerizing. She becomes Kern's steady date at Valley View College.

The most remarkable colored beauty of them all is Samuella "Sammy" Thompson. On the one hand, Savoy emphasizes her rage and boldness in frankly relating how she and two other Valley View coeds are accosted by some local Alabama rednecks. On the other hand, for reasons not entirely clear, Savoy also wants us to admire how sexy Sammy is when she is angry. Not to be overlooked in Savoy's rendering of this performance, which pointedly takes place in the college's theater, the Playhouse, is Sammy's mixed-race heritage ("Hagar has contributed to Sammy's blood"), her connection to economic power ("I am going home to my daddy's lumber company, and every goddam Southerner he has working there is going to get the boot"), and her mobility ("this child of Hagar is leaving here as soon as money comes by wire"). All this, combined with certain natural endowments, makes Sammy the hottest woman in the novel: "Pushing her flaming red hair angrily back from her ears, green eyes flashing, her full figure tense with excitement and anger, she seemed older and more mature than her listeners—as mature as she actually was."

Later, after her account of wrestling free from the "ragged peckerwoods," we are told that Sammy "pressed her clenched fists tight against her hips, her breasts rising and falling with her deep stormy breathing." Mac Rodgers, the drama coach, chastises Sammy for not acting more ladylike, but that doesn't seem to be the point. The point is that Sammy is neither a lady nor a girl (even African American literature is full of both) but a (newly created albeit fantasized) Woman. Hence, when she gets right up in Rodgers's face and tells him that she is a "big girl" who is absolutely certain that leaving Alabama isn't running away but *leaving*, Kern Roberts listens carefully. This is the very thing he should be able to say to his father, but can't manage to say, when he determines his own flight from the South.

Most central to *Alien Land*—and to African American literary history—is how Savoy advances the modern fictive project (which we first associate with James Weldon Johnson and his ex–colored man) of presenting a mixed-race protagonist who is male, not female. Much of what is new in the novel is generated by one simple reversal of expectations: in Savoy's plot the white parent is the mother and the black parent the father. What this means, at very least, is that the maternal ties that indelibly bind the protagonist to his colored mother and her race in so many other preceding fictions function here to explain Kern's loyalty to his white mother and forebears. *Alien Land* ends with Kern, Marianne, and daughter Margaret (as noted, named in memory of Kern's *maternal* white grandmother) residing in Vermont, the ancestral land of Laura Roberts, his mother. One senses that Kern has been journeying there ever since his mother died and he discovered that he could only find peace in his father's house when he retreated to his mother's private rooms.

Charles Roberts is the black parent—the black father—but neither phrase neatly sums him up, in part because he is also a mixed-race protagonist. Indeed, one way to think of Charles (with literary history as a guide) is to see him as the familiar mixed-race character (white father, black mother) who, in Savoy's novel, does two extraordinary things: he chooses to be, first, a black man and, second, a race man and to align himself with race men (Douglass, Du Bois, et al.) while helping to found the Freedom League (to be likened to the NAACP); and he fathers Kern, the new mixed-race character (black father, white mother). According to the preferred narrative among African Americans, Charles has made the right, heroic choice in becoming a race man. However, for Savoy, ever the modernist, this does not mean that Charles is flawless. He is distant as a husband, cold and nearly violent as a father, and devoted to his work to a dangerous degree. Charles is, as the *New York Times* review opined, "self-righteous." At times, his self-righteousness is a form of insanity. In a novel full of angry, maddened plebeian black men, Charles is the educated colored crazy. That in itself renders the reconciliation at the end between Charles and Kern difficult to applaud. In part, we worry about Kern and his family: *which* Charles is about to visit them in Vermont?

Willard Savoy continued writing after the publication of *Alien Land* and completed a novel, entitled, at least for a time, *Michael Gordon,* which was summarily rejected in 1954 and 1955. According to Savoy's records, his novel was unacceptable because it " 'attacked' a then 'sacred cow'—Washington D. C. in the earliest stages of de-segregation and school integration." Savoy was also told that he had written, as one editor put it, "an angry, bitter, hopeless and untrue story." Timing is everything, and the rejection of Savoy's *Michael Gordon* in the mid-1950s may well have had more to do with McCarthyism, the Cold War, and the *Brown v. Board of Education* decision than with anything inherently wrong with Savoy's new novel. Then, too, it may well be that Savoy was still writing in the 1950s a certain kind of angry, protest 1940s novel that seemed particularly out of date, especially after Ralph Ellison's *Invisible Man* was published to widespread acclaim in 1952. Who can be sure?

What we do know is that *Alien Land,* the novel Willard Savoy did publish, is remarkable as a mid-twentieth-century reinvention of the "passing" novel. Moreover, it is also remarkable as a midcentury protest novel, complete with portraits of how fatal violence and freighted courtroom deliberations, north and south, affect the lives of complex, racially mixed people. Savoy was always thinking forward, convinced that the next book would prove to kith and kin what he was worth. He should have been more satisfied with *Alien Land* than he seemed to be: it is a gift to his parents and to his wife and daughter, and certainly a fascination for students of American literature.

ACKNOWLEDGMENTS

This essay was originally published, in much the same form, as the foreword to the 2006 reprint of Willard Savoy's *Alien Land* (1949: reprint,

Hanover, N.H.: University Press of New England, 2006). I thank Richard Yarborough and Ellen Wicklum for their considerable help and generosity while we worked on that project. I thank Lauret Savoy for urging the republication of her father's novel, and for sharing with me all sorts of documents related to the first publication of *Alien Land,* including announcements, reviews, photographs, her father's correspondence and his private journal entries. These remarkable materials greatly assisted my work on this essay.

AFTERWORD

Distrust of the Reader in Afro-American Narratives

> You know everything. . . . A black mama birthed you, let you suck her titty, cleaned your dirty drawers, and you still look at us through paper and movie plots. . . . "Now this is the way it happened." . . . I want you to *write* it on whatever part of your brain that ain't already covered with page print.
>
> —James Alan McPherson, "The Story of a Scar"

One does not have to read very far into the corpus of Afro-American letters to find countless examples of the exaltation of literacy and the written word. In Frederick Douglass's *Narrative* of 1845, he proclaims that learning his "A, B, C"—and overhearing that, as a slave, he wasn't supposed to—was his "pathway from slavery to freedom." In Frances E. W. Harper's "Sketches of Southern Life" (1872), the persona of the "Aunt Chloe" poem, "Learning to Read," declares:

> So I got a pair of glasses,
>   And straight to work I went,
> And never stopped till I could read
>   The hymns and Testament.
>
> Then I got a little cabin,
>   A place to call my own—
> And I felt as independent
>   As a queen upon her throne.

Du Bois's *Souls of Black Folk* (1903) offers many eloquent testimonials to literacy, including the famous passage that begins "I sit with Shakespeare and he winces not." Richard Wright's *Black Boy* (1945) is essentially the chronicle of how, as a youth, the author/persona "burned to learn to read," partly so that he might leave the South for a full, literate life upon "undreamed-of shores of knowing." Such examples appear in every period; somewhere in the canon of nearly every Afro-American writer, literacy is extolled and the written word minted as the coin of freedom's realm.

In *From Behind the Veil* particularly, I have argued that the Afro-American quest for freedom has been more precisely a quest for freedom *and* literacy—and that this dual quest has provided not just a subject but a narrative structure for much of the culture's written literature. There is a decided value to this argument: it enables discussion of the literature and culture alike in literary terms. But my focus here is quite different, not opposed but broader and dialectical. What I will argue here is that Afro-American literature has developed as much because of the culture's distrust of literacy as because of its abiding faith in it.

Let me begin with two of literacy's most fervent advocates, Frederick Douglass and Richard Wright. In the years just after the publication of his great *Narrative,* Douglass encountered hostility from friend and foe alike, apparently because of his increasing skills as a speaker and writer. In his autobiography *My Bondage and My Freedom,* he tells us that friends urged that he confine his acts of literacy to the narrow straits of what they insisted was his story, while foes declared in so many words that his literacy in and of itself made them suspect that neither his story nor Douglass himself existed. It was in response to his foes, but possibly to his friends as well, that Douglass soon composed the *Narrative.* But recall: these annoying encounters with censorship of one form or another proved to be grist not for the *Narrative* but for the autobiography still to come. While it was Douglass's audience's distrust of him that led to the *Narrative,* it was his increasing distrust of *them* that prompted *My Bondage* as well as his newspapers, his novella, "The Heroic Slave," and his removal, in fine American form, to the "West" (Rochester, N.Y.). In short, the illiteracy of the allegedly literate spurred Douglass the speaker to become also Douglass the writer and editor.

Richard Wright's career at times shows remarkable parallels to Douglass's. In what both men choose to recall of their early years in their autobiographies, the effort to gain literacy is a subject matched only by that of how each had to cloak or disavow his skills once even a measure of literacy was attained. The incidents they recall in this regard are often strikingly similar: at some point each had to find whites who were sufficiently unsuspecting to impart lessons or advice; each had to endure the distrust from and occasional betrayals by fellow blacks; each had to hide the few books he had. For each, youth was a time in which one had to learn how to perform, as it were, before unreliable audiences, white and black, especially if one aspired to a condition of literacy that, if realized and inadvertently displayed, would render those audiences all the more distrustful and hostile.

What Douglass and Wright learned as black youths in the South was just as useful to them once each gained a degree of freedom in the North. For all the obvious differences, personal and cultural, there are significant parallels between Wright's experiences among the American Communists and Douglass's among New England's abolitionists. The censoring of Wright by the Communists, for example, is unquestionably of a piece with the censorship to which the Garrisonians subjected Douglass. In both cases, sympathizers, men and women who strove to see through race to the individual and to champion that individual's right to free access to literacy, became confused about the distinction between employing and exploiting an individual as a race representative. And in both cases, they were also confused about whether access to literacy for that individual was to be for their purposes or those that the individual might construe. When one thinks of how Douglass's newspapers were soon blacklisted by the Garrisonians and of how Wright was barred from Communist May Day parades, it is not difficult to see why Douglass removed to the West or why Wright expatriated to France. Friends found on "undreamed-of shores" had turned out to be the most distrustful sort of unfriendly natives.

Just as Douglass wrote his *Narrative* in response to his audience's distrust of him, so Wright composed *Uncle Tom's Children* (1938) and *Twelve Million Black Voices* (1941) partly to appease the distrust he encountered from blacks and whites alike once he came North. Similarly, Douglass's many writerly activities of the 1850s express *his* distrust of those who distrusted him, while Wright increasingly vented his own distrust of the American left, first in "Blueprint for Negro Literature" (1937), then in *Native Son* (1940), and finally in the whole of *American Hunger,* of which only the first section, *Black Boy,* was published in 1945. More specifically, *My Bondage and My Freedom* revises the *Narrative* in accord with Douglass's distrust of his audience, much as the whole of *American Hunger* (that is, the original manuscript) revises *Black Boy.*

For the most part, distrust of the American reader prompted Douglass and Wright to write and affected the choices they made regarding what they would write about. Distrust motivated them to improve their writing skills and to venture into new areas of inquiry and writerly performance, including those that were designated by custom, ideology, and an implicit racism the provinces of others. (In *American Hunger,* for example, Wright asks, "Didn't Lenin read bourgeois books?" and a "comrade" replies, "But you're not Lenin.") Once we consider distrust of the American reader and of American acts of reading to be a primary and pervasive motivation for Afro-American writing, we are equipped to read the autobiographies of Douglass, Wright, and many other writers in fresh and useful ways. This distrust is not merely a subject or theme of certain autobiographies. Nor is it something that exists in some festering form within the writer, or within his or her act of writing as distinct from the resulting texts. While distrust prompts some Afro-American writers to write about almost anything and everything, it has led others to write about distrust itself—to create and refine what I call a *discourse of distrust*. In short, a study of distrust in Afro-American writing can (and should) lead to new perceptions of the various strains and historical contours within Afro-American literature as a whole.

In the following section I offer a few of my thoughts in this regard, principally by choosing to see the distinction between distrusting writers who write and those who write about their distrust as being more precisely that between storywriters and (writing) storytellers. Part of what allows this last distinction is the requisite presence, and frequently active role, of the distrusting American reader—thinly guised as an unreliable story listener—in storytelling texts. With this in view, I then raise questions about the adequacies of the "social models" for reader-response literary analysis, especially since they do not seem to be, in Du Bois's terms, "frank and fair" about the American "race rituals" that invariably affect American acts of reading. In the concluding section I describe the narrative strategies of several storytelling texts, mostly contemporary ones, to provide thereby a morphology of the Afro-American storytelling narrative.

The Afro-American discourse of distrust assumes many narrative forms and infiltrates many literary genres. My focus here is not on the autobiographical or confessional modes of this literature (for example, the Douglass and Wright autobiographies), or on literary essays such as Ralph Ellison's "World and the Jug"— which is justly famous in part because it so eloquently expresses Ellison's distrust of Irving Howe as a reader of modern black fiction. Nor will I turn to poems such as Gwendolyn Brooks's "Negro Hero" or Michael Harper's "Nightmare Begins Responsibility," even though both poems are major texts largely because they portray how a "distrusting [black] self" may cope with that self as well as with those "audiences" that "read" him or her, often cavalierly or distrustingly. My concern is instead with fiction and with coming to some understanding of why some Afro-American storywriters and novelists distrust the term "fiction" and choose to see themselves as storytellers instead of storywriters, even though they can hardly surmount the fact that they *are* writing, and that simulations of storytelling performances in written art are, no matter how artful, simulations and little more. In the texts of these writers, distrust is not so much a subject as a basis for specific narrative plottings and rhetorical strategies. Moreover, these texts are fully "about" the communicative prospects of Afro-Americans writing for American readers, black and white, given the race rituals that color reading and/or listening. If we can understand these prospects, we can have a surer sense of how American culture is developing and in what direction.

The effort to draw a distinction between storytelling and story-writing in a written Afro-American literature is by no means unique on my part. Authors and critics alike have engaged in this task for years. Novelist Gayl Jones, for example, remarked in a 1975 interview,

> for me fiction and storytelling are different. I say I'm a fiction writer if I'm asked, but I really think of myself as a storyteller. When I say "fiction," it evokes a lot of different kinds of abstractions,

but when I say "storyteller," it always has its human connections. . . . There is always that kind of relationship between a storyteller and a hearer—the seeing of each other. The hearer has to
see/hear the storyteller, but the storyteller has to see/hear the
hearer, which the written tradition doesn't usually acknowledge.[1]

What Jones attempts to describe here is a mode, if not exactly a
genre, in written narrative that accommodates the performative
aesthetic of oral storytelling by fashioning characters (voices)
who pose as tellers and hearers and occasion thereby certain
types of narrative structuring. In acknowledging and discussing
this mode, several Afro-Americanist scholars have produced a
useful intrinsic criticism of storytelling within texts. I think here
of John F. Callahan's explorations of the "spoken in the written
word," Robert O'Meally's discussions of the written "preach-
erly" voice, and the recent studies that strive to make distinctions between black speech and literary dialect.[2]

However, I believe that Jones is making another point as
well, one that both complicates our notion of written storytelling and challenges us to discuss the texts in ways that are not
exclusively intrinsic. Jones suggests that storytelling narratives
not only present voices as tellers and hearers but also coerce
authors and readers (or, if you will, texts and readers) into teller-
hearer relationships. In other words, storytelling narratives create "interpretive communities"[3] in which authors, texts, and
readers collectively assert that telling and hearing may be occasioned by written tales and that the distinctions between telling
and writing, on the one hand, and hearing and reading, on the
other, are far more profound than they are usually determined
to be in those interpretive groupings constituted by other types
of fictive narrative.

The role of the reader is the key issue here, and not just because examinations of the reader require new, less intrinsic ap-

proaches to storytelling texts. I would submit that the reader in the storytelling paradigm is what makes that model different. Many models accommodate rather easily the idea of an author or text "telling" a story, but only the storytelling paradigm posits that readers, in "constituting" themselves through engaging the text, become hearers, with all that that implies in terms of how one may sustain through reading the *responsibilities* of listenership as they are defined in purely performative contexts. In reading experiences occasioned by storytelling texts, the reader may be an "implied," "informed," or "competent" figure, as Wolfgang Iser, Stanley Fish, and Jonathan Culler have declared the engaged readers of most written traditions to be.[4] But within the storytelling interpretive community, implication (especially insofar as it embraces complicity), knowledge, and competency are all measured according to a different scale. That scale measures hearing, not reading, the distinction being most apparent when the acts of authoring that hearing and reading spawn are compared.

To speak of the authoring a reader performs is to refer as well to the risks assumed when a reader is invited to partake in either type of communicative event. The written traditions that encourage fiction-making incite competitive authoring; readers of these writerly texts author competing texts both when they attempt to articulate what the prompting text means (or what its author intends) and when they go the other, "deconstructionist route" and playfully mime the prompting text's apparent deviousness or meaninglessness. In either case, the risk undertaken is that the prompting text will be rightfully or wrongfully superseded by one of its competing offspring—as countenanced, of course, by the jury of "informed" authors engendered by text. Glory and probable canonization come either through angst or anxiety. In the first scenario, the reader is in varying degrees defeated as an author but left with the consolation of knowing that the competing text he or she can imagine (but not yet or perhaps ever fully render) has at least a pedagogic or scholarly value. In the second scenario, the reader is characteristically triumphant as an author, which is to say that the prompting text has entered the firmament precisely because its authorship has been not so much passed along as conquered. In either case, the prompting text "lives" because its authorship has been contested.

Competition of a kind occurs in storytelling, but most of the communicative impulses within that tradition discourage competition of the order found in most written traditions, and risk is defined in new terms. While fiction-making and its kindred activities incite competitive authoring, storytelling invites comparable authoring; the "hearer" within the storytelling model is encouraged to compose what are essentially authenticating texts for the prompting story narrative.[5] What this means in part is that competition within the model is largely a matter of hearers vying with hearers as authenticators, and not one of readers attempting to create through their "reading" a stronger text than that which initiated their interpretive community. The risks that written storytelling undertakes are thus at least twofold: one is that the reader will become a hearer but not manage an authenticating response; the other is that the reader will *remain a reader* and not only belittle or reject storytelling's particular "keen disturbance"[6] but also issue confrontational responses that sustain altogether different definitions of literature, of literacy, and of appropriate reader response. The threat to most texts in the written tradition is that readers will cause them to swerve; the threat to a storytelling text is that readers will hasten its death.

While the risks to written storytelling are just this high, the rewards are equally great, especially in terms of the opportunities provided for authors and texts alike to be an advancing force within various literary traditions *and* a subversive factor within them as well. Subversion is probably most apparent in storytelling's persistent efforts to sustain the tenets of a performative aesthetic in an artistic medium ostensibly hostile to that aesthetic. Consider, for example, how subversive it is for storytelling to pursue various explicitly didactic strategies ("Now this is the way it happened. . . . I want you to *write* it on whatever part of your brain that ain't already covered with page print.") in an era in which most critics proclaim that "true art ignores the audience"[7] and most writers write accordingly. Subversion is also apparent in the previously discussed notion that the competent reader must become a competent *hearer* who eventually tells authenticating stories, especially since it is obviously "bad form" for any author or text to insist upon that degree of "submission" as an element of reading well. However, the most subversive, and hence most interesting, claim that storytelling makes is that, contrary to what most modern critics and even some writers tell us, it is the reader—not the author or text and certainly not the storyteller in the text—who is unreliable.

Most theories of creative reading and/or authoring offer episodes in which a devious or elusive text is grappled, if not altogether subdued, by a comparably ingenious reader. All such assaults are rationalized as a necessary, creative activity: it is the reader's lot to control or "reauthor" a text, which, by its taunting deviousness or playfulness—its *unreliability*—has actually invited the reader's aggression. Storytelling seeks to turn this model inside out. In Afro-American storytelling texts especially, rhetoric and narrative strategy combine time and again to declare that the principal unreliable factor in the storytelling paradigm is the reader (white American readers, obviously, but blacks as well) and that acts of creative communication are fully initiated, not when the text is assaulted but when the reader gets "told"—or "told off"—in such a way that he or she finally begins to *hear*. It is usually in this way that most written tales express their distrust, not just of readers but of official literate culture in general.[8] It is also in this way that they sustain the instructional nature of performed storytelling in a cultural context that devalues didactic art.

Wayne Booth has written: "Much of our scholarly and critical work of the highest seriousness has . . . employed . . . [a] dialectical opposition between artful showing and inartistic, merely rhetorical, telling."[9] It should not be surprising, then, to find that in American literary studies, the biographical studies of Mark Twain are generally superior to the critical studies of his works, that the many fine examinations of Faulkner and Ellison usually minimize their subversive activities as storytellers, and that within the realm of Afro-American letters alone, the studies of storywriters (for example, Wright and Baldwin) are both more voluminous and more thoughtful than those of storytellers (Gaines, McPherson, and Jones).[10] And so we must ask how literary history may be reconstituted to accommodate the storytelling strain in its own right.

The challenge occurs on two fronts: the intrinsic analysis of what is most minimally conceived to be the text, and the extrinsic analysis of what might be termed the text seen "large," that is, the text performing itself as well as its subversive activities. In the first case, the scholar of written literatures must consider the extent to which current *oral* literature theories illuminate the inner workings of a written text. These theories are primarily structuralist and thereby immune (for the most part) to the seductions of ferreting out intrinsic meaning or intention. New approaches to the text (and to literary history) also occur because most of the oral literature theories proceed from assumptions regarding the contextual origins of oral stories (and storytelling) that yield a critical language that usefully examines written tales as well.[11] What oral literature scholars mean in their use of familiar terms such as "theme" and "repetition" is often different from what scholars of written literatures mean, and those differences encourage fresh approaches to written literatures. To argue, for example, as Albert Lord did some thirty years ago, that a theme is not so much a "central or dominating idea" as a repeated incident or description—a "narrative building block"—is to confront most literary scholars with a new idea of thematic criticism.[12] Similarly, Harold Scheub's notion that narrative repetition finds its form in "expansible and patterned and parallel image-sets" usefully takes one beyond conventional considerations of the reiterated word or phrase or of the re-worded idea.[13] Generally, what the oral literature scholars provide are methods and terms for critical discourse on the large units of narrative structure—the "macro-units," if you will—that most readily identify tales as the distilled products of various artistic impulses both collected and controlled. Since even the written Afro-American tale is similarly multigeneric in intention and often in result, it is also open to "macronic" analysis.

Regarding the extrinsic analysis of written storytelling, I should acknowledge at once that what I have just described as an intrinsic method could equally be seen as extrinsic. Oral literature scholars always assume that narratives are performed art forms and accordingly view the written texts of narratives as necessary but altogether limited approximations of complex events. When David Buchan directs our attention to the stanzaic units in Scottish ballads rather than to the stanzas themselves, he does so because the clustering of stanzas into larger structural units has a far greater bearing on the production and reception of ballads than that of the stanza itself.[14] Buchan is aware of the solitary stanza's autonomy and authority on the printed page; yet he submits not to that authority but to that of stanzas-in-performance and fashions his narrative analysis accordingly. In sum, his intrinsic analysis is distinctly extrinsic.

Nonetheless, I find it useful to distinguish between discussions of narrative structure and those of reader or listener response, and to refer to these respectively as intrinsic and extrinsic critical discourse. Written tales present at least two challenges to most reader-response theories. One is offered by the framed tale readily found in both nineteenth- and twentieth-century Afro-American writing. Framed tales by their nature invent storylisteners within their narratives, and storyreaders, through their acts of reading, may be transformed into storylisteners. In tale after tale, considerable artistic energy is brought to the task of persuading readers to constitute themselves as listeners, the key issue affecting that activity being whether the reader is to pursue such self-transformations in accord with or at variance with the model of the listener found within the narrative itself. In other words, the competent reader of framed tales always must decide just how much he or she will or can submit to the model of listening that almost always is the dominating meta-plot of the tale. The reader must decide as well to what extent a refusal to submit endangers his or her competency.

What this suggests is that framed tales seem to require two kinds of "reader-response" analysis: one of teller-listener relations within the narrative, another of those relations incorporating the "outside" reader. Moreover, a full extrinsic study of a framed tale does not declare as supreme the latter analysis, as most reader-response theories aggressively do, but attempts to fashion an accommodation of both analyses. The challenge is to manage such accommodations.

Beyond this lies the specific challenge presented by the Afro-American framed tale in particular. In its depictions within narratives of demonstrably white or black listeners, and in its presumption that most of its readers are white (specifically, white Americans), the Afro-American framed tale confronts interracial and intraracial rituals of behavior while fashioning various models of readership. While these features invariably distinguish the Afro-American framed tale from other framed tales, they do not remove these tales from the mainstream of the Afro-American written story. Tales that aren't framed are much like those that are, especially since the narrating voices within them are normally those of whites or blacks who have undergone listenership and who are now attempting storytelling at a level comparable to that which first engaged their attention. Once we acknowledge as well that nonframed Afro-American tales also assume a white readership, we may say that, in their narrative intentions and recognition of communicative prospects, both types of written tales are far more candid than the reader-response literary critics have been about how acts of listening and reading may be complicated by race.

The second kind of challenge that written storytelling presents to reader-response theories is therefore obvious: to what extent are the psychological, intersubjective, and even social models of reader-response analysis articulate about the communicative situations black authors in the Americas have confronted for two hundred years? While something useful may be gleaned from all three models, the social models of Stanley Fish (in his most recent phase) and Steven Mailloux are the most useful, even though they are relatively underdeveloped for these purposes.[15]

Fish advances a sophisticated concept of the "authority" invested in interpretive communities by acts of reading, which is useful, for example, in suggesting how written tales manage authority in simulated performative communities. On the other hand, he seems rather naïve about interpretive arbitration within those bodies comprising readership on a large scale. Mailloux criticizes Fish's notion of interpretive communities for referring only to "one aspect (though a most important one) of historical communities—shared constitutive conventions for making sense of reality" (137). He argues, "More often, however, historical communities are made up of several conflicting interpretive communities" (137), from which I infer that Mailloux envisions America as being made up of many historical *and* interpretive communities often contending with each other over the prime issues of which conventions are shared and which render the world real.

However, one must ask—as Afro-Americanists always must ask of Americanists—which working definition of community underlies Mailloux's assertion? I say "working" because quite often the bone of contention between Afro-Americanists and Americanists is less a matter of pure definition than one of how terms are put to use. For example, it is difficult to find fault with Mailloux's claim that "common ties remain the most relevant general criteria for defining community," or with what he understands "common ties" to be: "shared traditions, imposed or agreed upon behavior patterns, and common ways of making sense—that is, as traditional, regulative, and constitutive conventions" (137). However, where these thoughts lead Mailloux is, I think, a curious matter, especially in light of his posture as a revisionist literary historian.

After usefully citing Jessie Bernard's definition of communities as " 'clubs' whose conventions constitute a kind of boundary-maintenance device," Mailloux then argues that "the historical communities that fill the category of 'literature' can be whole societies, but more often they are societal groups based on economic organization (for example, the network of authors, publishers, periodical editors, and book reviewers), social rank (for instance, intelligentsia and governing classes), or institutional and professional position (such as English professor)" (137–138). What is exposed here is the bare outline of an all too familiar story: intentionally or not, another Americanist is shying away from confronting the role that race has played in America in creating communities (black *and* white) veritably bristling with traditional, regulative, and constitutive conventions. Should Mailloux argue that racial societal groups in America are not as pertinent or substantial as those based on economic organization, social rank, or professional position, he would be sadly mistaken. Should he contend instead that America's racial societal groups have not "filled" the category of American literature, he would be more mistaken still. In either case, Mailloux offers no guidance on this considerable issue. Just as his new readings of Hawthorne, Melville, and Crane are illuminating but in no way reflective of the *many* historical and interpretive communities in nineteenth-century America, his social model for what might be called the American act of reading is insufficiently social.

It is quite possible that the most useful, amending model—useful especially in terms of comprehending the abiding link in America between race and readership—is to be found in rough form within the aggregate literature of the Afro-American written tale. We must therefore attempt to extract and formalize the social mode of reading collectively authored by Afro-American writers as various as Frederick Douglass, Charles Chesnutt, Jean Toomer, Zora Neale Hurston, Ralph Ellison, Ernest Gaines, Toni Morrison, Gayl Jones, James Alan McPherson, Alice Walker, and David Bradley. In doing so, we should be less concerned with offering a chronology or even a history of Afro-American literature based upon those authors than with suggesting how the "basic" written tale has been modified over time, usually in an effort to accommodate the changing subtleties of America's race rituals, so that appropriately revised models of competent readership can be advanced.

The basic written tale is fundamentally a framed tale in which either the framed or framing narrative depicts a black storyteller's white listener socially and morally maturing into competency. In thus presenting a very particular reader in the text, the basic written tale squarely addresses the issue of its probable audience while raising an issue for some or most of its readers regarding the extent to which they can or will identify with the text's "reader" while pursuing (if not always completing) their own act of reading. Where matters develop beyond this is the subject of the next section.

Let me begin by noting that while there are many white storytellers throughout the Afro-American written canon, they are always novices—freshly elevated to the rank of teller by virtue of their newly acquired competency as listeners—and never master storytellers. Many black storytellers, especially in modern and contemporary narratives, also are novices, but a few (Charles Chesnutt's Uncle Julius, Ernest Gaines's Miss Jane Pittman, David Bradley's Old Jack Hawley) are master storytellers, custodians of the prompting tales. They seem to pass from knowing to possessing the tales (as a curator "possesses" a fine painting) as they share them. We may thus recognize several tale types that are created by the presence or absence in narratives of master tellers, novice tellers, and unreliable listeners in varying combinations, and by the positioning of these figures as primary or ancillary tellers or listeners in narratives as wholes. The accompanying chart will be of assistance here.

Type A stories are the basic tales in the written storytelling tradition. By "basic" I do not mean that they are primitive or unsophisticated, or that they are numerically dominant within the canon. Rather, these are the stories in which (a) the primary narrators are black master storytellers, (b) tales of a didactic nature are told to conspicuously incompetent listeners, largely out of distrust of them, (c) the listeners are fully present as characters or voices and not as "implied" personages, (d) the tales within the stories are autobiographical only insofar as they partake of episodes from the master teller's personal history, and (e) the framed-tale structure of the narrative as a whole is fully intact and seemingly inviolate.

Type A and A' stories differ in terms of the race of the listener—and hence in terms of the stated or implied performative context in which the master teller's tale is told. The story types also differ as to the frequency with which they are composed as discrete written stories. While a number of type A stories appear in the canon as full-fledged narratives—such as James Alan McPherson's story "Problems of Art"—they emerge more often as the tales within the type B story cited in the chart. In contrast, type A' stories frequently are discrete stories. McPherson's stories "Solo Song: For Doc" and "The Story of a Scar" enhance this category, as does Hurston's novel *Their Eyes Were Watching God.*

Type B tales are told by novice storytellers who have just recently achieved competency as listeners. This fact is important, for it explains why the tale offered is basically an account of the storytelling event that occasioned the novice teller's competency, and why the master teller *and* his or her tale fully dominate that account. In other words, the novice teller is seemingly still too close to the moment when competency was achieved and too overwhelmed by the teller, tale, and other features of that moment to author a story that is anything other than a strict account of that moment.

The characteristics of type B (and B') stories are therefore as follows: (a) although the story's primary narrator is a novice teller (white or black), the black master teller is fully present as the teller of the story's tale; (b) although the novice teller may tell the tale of his or her previous incompetency to listeners situated within the tale's frame, direct address to the "listener" outside the story (the "outside" reader) is both possible and likely; (c) although the predominating autobiographical statement is

STORYTELLERS AND TALES IN AFRO-AMERICAN FRAMED TALES

Type A: basic story	Type A': basic story with black listener
Master teller to white listener, usually with veiled instructions for listener	Master teller to black listener, usually with veiled instructions for listener
Type B: novice story 1 basic novice story	Type B': novice story 1 basic novice story with black novices
White novice teller to readers = basic story A	Black novice teller to readers = basic story A'
Type C: novice story 2	Type C': novice story 2 with black novice
White novice teller to readers = framing narrative of basic story A	Black novice teller to readers = framing narrative of basic story A'
Type D: novice story 3	Type D': novice story 3 with black novice
White novice teller to readers = type C tale varied without master teller	Black novice teller to readers = type C tale varied without master teller

still that offered by the master teller in the tale, the novice tell-er's self-history also has a place, sometimes a significant one, in the story as a whole; (d) although the story is normally a framed tale, with this type we begin to see improvisations on that struc-ture, especially in those instances where the story is repeated and otherwise developed for the needs and purposes of novellas and novels.

Two points must be stressed here, both involving story fea-tures that the basic novice's story initiates. One is that the nov-ice teller's story is essentially autobiographical; the other is that his or her act of composing the narrative whole is a form of what I have described before as comparable storytelling. What makes the basic novice's story "basic" is that both of these features are pursued at an elementary level. Invariably, a single episode passes for autobiography, and repetition of the master teller's tale—albeit with some record of how the teller, when a listener, thwarted and/or abetted a given performance of the tale—passes for comparable telling. Once we see that these resolutions to the two most basic impulses within the novice's story are the obvious resolutions, we can also see why at least two more types of novice stories have developed. There is room in the form for a larger measure of the novice teller's autobiography and room as well for acts of comparable telling that exclude the master teller and do not repeat any of his or her specific tales. This is not to say that type B stories are unremarkable; Douglass's sole fiction, "The Heroic Slave," and Charles Chesnutt's Uncle Julius stories are type B stories, and the type B' category includes such estimable texts as Ernest Gaines's *Autobiography of Miss Jane Pittman*, Hurston's *Mules and Men*, McPherson's "Story of a Dead Man," and Gayl Jones's *Corregidora*. However, these stories offer but one solution to how one may create a written art out of the storytelling event most accurately simulated in story types A and A'.

I have devised story type C chiefly to acknowledge that for some novice tellers the event (or events) of storytelling that initiated their transformation from listeners to tellers may be appropriately recognized and recounted without full reference to the tale the master teller told at that time. The tale is thus incidental to the event in some accounts; in others, no one tale stands out as central to the former listener's epiphanic experience. In the type C story, the master teller is nonetheless on the scene, though full versions of his or her story are not. This means that his or her presence in the type C story is often more figurative than literal.

These economies in the rendering of master teller and master tale alike are usually to some major purpose. In Chesnutt's story "The Dumb Witness," reducing the presence of Julius (the master teller) and of his version of the tale leaves a space that John (the novice teller) fills with fragments of the tale he himself has collected. On the other hand, in the "Kabnis" section of Jean Toomer's *Cane*, the great effect of Father John (the master teller) saying so little so cryptically is that the novice/persona can be that much more autobiographical in his account of the advent of his competency. In either case, the larger role the novice plays in telling every aspect of the story leads to certain manipulations or dismantlings of the basic framed-tale structure. "The Dumb Witness" is a framed tale, but the fact that John's voice dominates both the frame and the tale means that, in this particular Julius story, we cannot distinguish between the frame and the tale in terms of what Alan Dundes and other folklorists would call "linguistic textures." Toomer's "Kabnis" modifies the storytelling story in precisely the opposite way. While the encounter with Father John is framed, and while differing vernaculars or textures are employed to distinguish his voice from that of the novice (and from those of the other figures assembled), there quite simply is no tale of any expected sort residing within either the frame or the language presumably created for tale telling.

These developments suggest that a new concept of comparable authoring emerges in the type C story. The manipulation of the framed-tale structure, diminution of the master tale, and virtual transformation of the master teller from voice to trope all seem to constitute acts of authorial competition; but I would contend that each of these activities is pursued in an effort to create a story that authenticates the essentials or essences of storytelling instead of the details of any one story or story event. The framed-tale structure is manipulated so that the novice teller may confirm in a fresh way that *telling grows out of listening*. Both acts are nearly simultaneously initiated by the acquisition of competency. Such confirmations may be possible in story types A and B, but they are far better managed in structures that do not segregate acts of telling from those of listening to the degree commonly found in rigidly executed framed tales. Moreover, the cost of reducing or deleting the master tale is willingly paid if the result is a self-portrait of the novice teller that persuades us that something more has been accomplished on the order of cultural integration (or reintegration) than that of tale memorization.

This feature yields our best clue as to why the master teller appears more as trope than voice. Something has to embody the historical and/or interpretive community of which the novice teller is now presumably a part, and of which he or she now tells stories. That "something" is commonly the master teller, who, in one sense, began the whole business. If the pursuit of these activities in a type C story fashions a narrative that authenticates the communal context from which master teller and tale alike emerge, and that authenticates as well the essential oneness of context, teller, and tale, then it is a good and comparable story within the tradition. If any of this is mismanaged, the aesthetics of storytelling counsel us to receive the novice teller not as a promising competitive author but as one who is still at base an unreliable listener. This is one of the several points at which the aesthetics of storytelling also urge us to subvert our usual critical habits, for the disapproval with which we are to greet the erring novice is also to be freely bestowed on his or her author.

Much of the description just offered for the type C story holds for the type D story as well. However, the type D story attempts comparable storytelling without the outward presence of a master teller in a narrative. What this generally means is that the historical and/or interpretive community embodied by the master teller is configured in different but comparable terms. "Comparable" is a key word here. This is not just because we are discussing modes of comparable storytelling; it is essential to see that in these stories configurations such as family, kin, menfolk, womenfolk, the neighborhood, the Black Belt, the South, the ghetto, our people, and home (among others) occupy much the same space in the story that a master teller solely occupies in a type C tale. Indeed, one might say that they are identical to the master teller as signs for the same referent. However, this does not mean that master tellers are altogether absent from these stories. In many instances, it is impossible to evoke fully a given family, neighborhood, or "club" without acknowledging the storytellers who are unquestionably presences in the group. In other words, these storytellers no longer stand for the group as a whole, nor do they function as intermediaries between the group and the novice. When and if they appear in type D stories as tropes, what they configure is not so much a community as one or more of that body's shared conventions. Moreover, insofar as mediation between a community and "outsiders" occurs, it is pursued in varying degrees of explicitness by the novice teller. Central to all such mediations, especially in the type D story, is the manner in which the novice first forges, then wields, and then at strategic moments forsakes *his or her* distrust of outsiders. In this respect above all others, the act of mediation is yet another aspect of an attempt to manage comparable authorship.

Much of this comes clear when one thinks of the luminous figures of the South—and especially of the palpable presence of Georgia—in Toomer's *Cane*. Zora Neale Hurston's all-black town of Eatonville also is a communal context for storytelling, as are the black enclaves in Toni Morrison's novels and the Louisiana plantations in the fiction of Ernest Gaines. Each of these communities offers an unusually rich display of nearly archetypal characters, including a fair number of estimable raconteurs. And yet each of these communities looms larger than any one master teller or tale, and indeed subsumes teller and tale alike while becoming in every sense the major presence in a type D story.

I am well aware, of course, that certain texts do not neatly fall into one of my four categories, or mischievously blur them. As is often the case, there is something to be learned from such exceptions to the rule. Most of these "problem" texts are very new—some written yesterday, as it were. Many of them are long narratives—novellas or novels. Many can be usefully described as long narratives that in some measure are long precisely because they *combine* the story types just described. The texts include such acclaimed titles as Toni Morrison's *Song of Solomon* (1977), James Alan McPherson's "Elbow Room" (1977), David Bradley's *Chaneysville Incident* (1981), and Alice Walker's *Color Purple* (1982). The combinations achieved are various and at times stunningly comprehensive. Bradley's novel, for example, traces the career of a young historian who, after forsaking his stacks of note cards (his totems of official literacy), is transformed into an increasingly reliable listener and then into a better and better storyteller. In this fashion, the novel combines key aspects of the B', C', and D' story types as it unfolds, only to become, rather remarkably, a type A basic written tale at its closure.

Stories of this sort figure in this discussion partly because they challenge my categories, but mostly because they confirm, in their storytelling *about* storytelling, that storytelling has developed its own store of artistic conventions. They are "artistic" conventions, not strictly "literary" ones, chiefly because they have their origins in both oral and written art-making—for example, in both the oral and written versions of Frederick Douglass's story of the slave revolt hero Madison Washington. When our contemporary writers employ these conventions, they acknowledge that a particular tradition in Afro-American writing exists, and, knowingly or not, they place themselves within it. In this way, the tradition endures, and necessarily complicates, in rich and complex ways, our thinking about the points of congruence between Afro-American and other Western literatures.

NOTES

INDEX

NOTES

1. Frederick Douglass, Barack Obama, and the Search for Patrimony

[1] Barack Obama, *Dreams from My Father: A Story of Race and Inheritance* (New York: Three Rivers Press, 1995), 76. All further page references are to this edition (D).

[2] Ralph Ellison, *Invisible Man* (1952; reprint, New York: Vintage, 1995), 6.

[3] David Samuels, "Invisible Man: How Ralph Ellison Explains Barack Obama," *New Republic,* October 22, 2008.

[4] Frederick Douglass, *My Bondage and My Freedom* (1855: reprint, New York: Dover, 1969), 38. All further page references are to this edition (MB).

[5] Saidiya V. Hartman, *Scenes of Subjection: Terror, Slavery, and Self-making in Nineteenth-century America* (New York: Oxford University Press, 1997).

2. W. E. B. Du Bois, Barack Obama, and the Search for Race

[1] The epigraph to this chapter is from Bonnie Angelo, "The Pain of Being Black: An Interview with Toni Morrison" (1989), in Danielle Guthrie-Taylor, ed., *Conversations with Toni Morrison* (Jackson: University Press of Mississippi, 1994), 258. Italics added.

[2] Rayford W. Logan, *The Negro in American Life and Thought: The Nadir, 1877–1901* (New York: Dial, 1954).

[3] W. E. B. Du Bois, *The Souls of Black Folk,* ed. David W. Blight and Robert Gooding-Williams (1903; reprint, Boston: Bedford, 1997), 38. All further page references are to this edition (S).

[4] See, for example, Shamoon Zamir, *Dark Voices: W. E. B. Du Bois and American Thought, 1888–1903* (Chicago: University of Chicago Press, 1995), 138.

⁵ James Weldon Johnson, *The Autobiography of an Ex–Colored Man* (1912; reprint, New York: Penguin, 1990), 6. All further page references are to this edition (ECM).

⁶ Donald Moss, "Introduction: On Hating in the First Person Plural: Thinking Psychoanalytically about Racism, Homophobia, and Misogyny," in Moss, ed., *Hating in the First Person Plural: Psychoanalytic Essays on Racism, Homophobia, Misogyny, and Terror* (New York: Other Press, 2003), xxxiii. All further references to this essay are shown as "H" followed by page number.

⁷ Zora Neale Hurston, *Their Eyes Were Watching God* (1937; reprint, New York: Harper Perennial, 1990), 8. All further page references are to this edition (T).

⁸ See Mary Helen Washington's summary of the critical response to Hurston from Sterling Brown, Alain Locke, and Richard Wright in her foreword (T vii–viii).

⁹ Barack Obama, *Dreams from My Father* (New York: Three Rivers Press, 1995), 54. All further page references are to this edition (D).

3. TONI MORRISON, BARACK OBAMA, AND DIFFERENCE

¹ The first epigraph to this chapter is from Toni Morrison, "Unspeakable Things Unspoken: The Afro-American Presence in American Literature" (1988), in James P. Draper, ed., *Black Literature Criticism* (Detroit: Gale Research, 1992), 3: 1433.

² The second epigraph to this chapter is from Barack Obama, *Dreams from My Father* (New York: Three Rivers Press, 1995), xi. All further page references are to this edition (D).

³ David Samuels, "Invisible Man: How Ralph Ellison Explains Barack Obama," *New Republic*, October 22, 2008.

⁴ Commentary from Morrison on the communities and neighborhoods in her novels, offered during the period in which she was writing *Song of Solomon*, appears in her 1976 interview with me. See Robert B. Stepto, " 'Intimate Things in Place': A Conversation with Toni Morrison," in Michael S. Harper and Robert B. Stepto, eds., *Chant of Saints: A Gathering of Afro-American Literature, Art, and Scholarship* (Urbana: University of Illinois Press, 1979), 214.

[5] Wendy Harding and Jacky Martin, *A World of Difference: An Intercultural Study of Toni Morrison's Novels* (Westport, Conn.: Greenwood Press, 1994). All further page references to this discussion are shown as "W" followed by page number.

[6] Toni Morrison, *Song of Solomon* (New York: Knopf, 1977), 29. All further page references are to this edition (SS).

[7] Jill Matus, *Toni Morrison* (Manchester: Manchester University Press, 1998), 79.

5. SHARING THE THUNDER

[1] "Stolen Thunder," *Frederick Douglass's Paper*, October 22, 1852, 2.

[2] Sue Eakin and Joseph Logsdon, introduction to Solomon Northup, *Twelve Years a Slave* (1853; reprint, Baton Rouge: Louisiana State University Press, 1968), xiv.

[3] Harriet Beecher Stowe to Frederick Douglass, July 9, 1851, in Charles Edward Stowe, ed., *Life of Harriet Beecher Stowe: Compiled from Her Letters and Journals* (Boston: Houghton Mifflin, 1890), 149–153.

[4] Gilbert Osofsky, ed., *Puttin' On Ole Massa* (New York: Harper and Row, 1969); Arna Bontemps, ed., *Great Slave Narratives* (Boston: Beacon Press, 1969); Robert B. Stepto, *From Behind the Veil: A Study of Afro-American Narrative* (Urbana: University of Illinois Press, 1979), 6–11.

[5] Herbert B. Gutman, *The Black Family in Slavery and Freedom, 1750–1925* (New York: Vintage Books, 1977), xxi.

[6] Henry Bibb, *Narrative of the Life and Adventures of Henry Bibb, an American Slave, Written by Himself*, in Osofsky, *Puttin' On Ole Massa*, 105.

[7] Ibid., 127.

[8] Ibid., 114.

[9] Ibid., 72.

[10] Ibid.

[11] Stowe to Douglass, July 9, 1851.

[12] Ibid.

[13] *Frederick Douglass's Paper*, November 19, 1852, 3. The announcement appears at least once again, on November 26, 1852.

[14] Frederick Douglass, "A Day and Night in 'Uncle Tom's Cabin,'" in Philip S. Foner, ed., *The Life and Writings of Frederick Douglass* (New York: International, 1950), 2: 227.

[15] Frederick Douglass, "Slavery the Life Issue: Addresses Delivered in Cincinnati, Ohio, on 11–13 April 1854," in John W. Blassingame, ed., *The Frederick Douglass Papers, Ser. 1, Speeches, Debates, and Interviews* (New Haven, Conn.: Yale University Press, 1982), 2:468.

[16] Frederick Douglass, "Bound Together in a Grand League of Freedom: An Address Delivered in Toronto, Canada West, on 21 June 1854," in Blassingame, *Frederick Douglass Papers, Ser. 1*, 1:495.

[17] Douglass, "Day and Night in 'Uncle Tom's Cabin,'" 227.

[18] Harriet Beecher Stowe, *Uncle Tom's Cabin*, ed. Kenneth Lynn (Cambridge, Mass.: Harvard University Press, 1962), chap. 4.

[19] Frederick Douglass, "The Heroic Slave," in Abraham Chapman, ed., *Steal Away: Stories of the Runaway Slaves* (New York: Praeger, 1971), 169.

[20] For additional remarks, see my "Storytelling in Early Afro-American Fiction: Frederick Douglass's 'The Heroic Slave,'" *Georgia Review* 36 (Summer 1982): 355–368.

[21] Douglass, "Heroic Slave," 151.

[22] Frederick Douglass to Harriet Beecher Stowe, March 8, 1853, in Foner, *Life and Writings of Frederick Douglass*, 2:233.

[23] Douglass, "Heroic Slave," 149.

[24] James Baldwin, "Everybody's Protest Novel," in Baldwin, *Notes of a Native Son* (1955; reprint, New York: Bantam, 1964), 9–17.

AFTERWORD

[1] Michael S. Harper, "Gayl Jones: An Interview," in Michael S. Harper and Robert B. Stepto, eds., *Chant of Saints: A Gathering of Afro-American Literature, Art, and Scholarship* (Urbana: University of Illinois Press, 1979), 355, 374–375.

[2] John F. Callahan, "Image-Making: Tradition and the Two Versions of the Autobiography of Miss Jane Pittman," *Chicago Review* 29 (Autumn 1977): 45–62, and *In the African-American Grain* (Urbana:

University of Illinois Press, 1988); Robert O'Meally, "The Text Was Meant to Be Preached," in Dexter Fisher and Robert B. Stepto, eds., *Afro-American Literature: The Reconstruction of Instruction* (New York: MLA, 1978); Myron Simon, "Dunbar and Dialect Poetry," in Jay Martin, ed., *A Singer in the Dawn: Reinterpretations of Paul Laurence Dunbar* (New York: Dodd, Mead, 1975), 114–134; Houston A. Baker, Jr., *The Journey Back: Issues in Black Literature and Criticism* (Chicago: University of Chicago Press, 1980), 1–52. This list is hardly inclusive and is only meant to be suggestive.

3 The phrase is Stanley Fish's; see his *Is There a Text in This Class?* (Cambridge, Mass.: Harvard University Press, 1980), esp. 171–173.

4 Wolfgang Iser, *The Implied Reader* (Baltimore: Johns Hopkins University Press, 1974); Stanley E. Fish, *Self-consuming Artifacts* (Berkeley: University of California Press, 1972); Jonathan Culler, *Structuralist Poetics* (Ithaca: Cornell University Press, 1975). Appropriate selections from these studies conveniently appear in Jane P. Tompkins, ed., *Reader-response Criticism* (Baltimore: Johns Hopkins University Press, 1980).

5 See my discussion of authenticating narratives in *From Behind the Veil* (Urbana: University of Illinois Press, 1979), 5, 26–31.

6 Iser's phrase; see Wolfgang Iser, "Indeterminacy and the Reader's Response," in J. H. Miller, ed., *Aspects of Narrative* (New York: Columbia University Press, 1971), 2.

7 Wayne C. Booth discusses this "truism" in *The Rhetoric of Fiction* (Chicago: University of Chicago Press, 1961), esp. in chap. 4, 89–116.

8 The "Americanness" of this Afro-American activity should be apparent. Mark Twain—to cite the most obvious example—also fashioned written tales expressing distrust of the reader and of the definitions of literacy represented by that reader. Indeed, it is fair to argue that some twentieth-century Afro-American writers (Sterling Brown and Ralph Ellison in particular) are in their storytelling as much American as Afro-American precisely because of their reading of Twain. But let us not lose sight of when this activity is distinctly "Afro-American" as well: while both traditions may pit teller against hearer in terms of

country versus city, South versus North, West versus East, common-sense versus booksense, and New World versus the Old, it is mainly, and perhaps exclusively, in Afro-American letters that this match may be fully played out across the ubiquitous net of America's color line.

[9] Booth, *Rhetoric of Fiction*, 27.

[10] The obvious exception is the rush of good work on Zora Neale Hurston.

[11] Part of my point here is that new concepts for the scholar of written literatures, such as Harold Scheub's theory of the expansible image, advance one's discussion of the written tale. See Scheub, "The Technique of the Expansible Image in Xhosa Ntsomi-Performances," *Research in African Literatures*, 1, 2 (1970): 119–146.

[12] Albert Lord, "Umbundu: A Comparative Analysis," in Merlin Ennis, ed., *Umbundu: Folktales from Angola* (Boston: Beacon Press, 1962), xvi.

[13] Scheub discusses narrative repetition at length in "Oral Narrative Process and the Use of Models," in Alan Dundes, ed., *Varia Folklorica* (The Hague: Mouton, 1978; reprint, Chicago: Aldine, 1978), 71–89. Also useful is his "Performance of Oral Narrative," in William R. Bascom, ed., *Frontiers of Folklore* (Boulder, Colo.: Westview Press, 1977), 54–78.

[14] David Buchan, *The Ballad and the Folk* (London: Routledge and Kegan Paul, 1972), 87–104.

[15] I refer to Fish's "most recent phase" because I distinguish between his concept of the early 1970s of the informed reader and his more recent idea of the interpretive community. See again his *Is There a Text in This Class?* (fn. 3). Regarding Mailloux, see his *Interpretive Conventions: The Reader in the Study of American Fiction* (Ithaca, NY: Cornell University Press, 1982), 126–139; further references are by page number in the text.

INDEX

by, 10, 12–14, 22–24, 26; on
literacy, 13–14, 16–17, 138,
139–140; on dreams of
freedom, 17–19; father figures
for, 17–19; religion and, 18,
20–21; on community,
19–22, 53; escape plans of,
20–21; escape of, 22–24;
name use by, 23–24; in
abolitionism, 24–26, 140–141;
on masculine beautify, 34; on
absent parents, 52; Stowe
and, 101–103; on geography
of freedom, 106; on African
colonization, 108; on the
church and slavery, 108; on
Stowe, 110–111; reader
distrust of, 140–142; social
reading mode and, 153. *See
also* "Heroic Slave, The"
(Douglass)
Dreams from My Father
(Obama), 12; on race and
identity, 7–9; on basketball,
19; schoolhouse episode
in, 27–28, 39–50; on
two-ness, 52
Du Bois, W. E. B., 31, 142;
schoolhouse episode of,
28–30; on the Veil, 29; on
double-consciousness, 52; on
geography of oppression, 127;
on literacy, 138–139
"Dumb Witness, The" (Chesnutt), 158

Dunbar, Paul Laurence, 20
Dundes, Alan, 158

"Elbow Room" (McPherson),
161
Ellison, Ralph, 8–9, 27, 136,
148; on masculine beauty,
34; reader distrust of, 143;
social reading mode and,
153
"Everybody's Protest Novel"
(Baldwin), 120

Fables, 60–70
Family: effects of slavery on,
9–12; Douglass on, 23–24;
Morrison on, 69–70; Stowe
on, 104–106, 107; Savoy on,
128–129, 134–135; biracial
identity and, 134–135. *See
also* Names
Fanon, Frantz, 132
Fathers, absent: Obama on, 7–8,
44–50; Douglass on, 10,
12–14, 17–19; Du Bois and,
35; Savoy on, 131; biracial
identity and, 134–135. *See
also* Family
Faulkner, William, 148
Fish, Stanley, 145, 151–152
Framed tales, 150–151,
153–154; story types of,
154–160